100 GREATEST EXPLORERS

DRAGON'S WORLD

DRAGON'S WORLD

CHILDREN'S BOOKS

Dragon's World Ltd
Limpsfield
Surrey RH8 0DY
Great Britain

First published by Dragon's World 1995

© Dragon's World 1995

Text: Michael Pollard
Editor: Kyla Barber
Copy Editor: Cathy Meeus
Designer: Mel Raymond
Design assistants: Karen Ferguson
                    Victoria Furbisher
Art Director: John Strange
Editorial Director: Pippa Rubinstein

The catalogue record for this book is available from the British Library

ISBN 1 85028 308 7

Printed in Italy

Contents

Introduction

Since our earliest days on earth, human beings have felt the need to find out more about the world in which we live. This book is about some of the people who have set out from their native lands on great journeys of exploration, always in danger and sometimes at the cost of their lives.

Why did they do it? Part of the answer is the thirst for adventure. Imagine looking at a view that no one has ever seen before, climbing a mountain that has never been climbed, or crossing a sea where no ship has ever sailed! Imagine being the very first human being to reach the South Pole or to set foot on the Moon!

It is not only the love of adventure that makes people explorers. Some, like the early explorers of Africa or Asia, were in search of new trading partners. Some, like the Spanish and Portuguese *conquistadores*, who laid claim to Central and South America over 400 years ago, were looking for gold, silver and precious stones. Others went in search of new routes to distant parts of the world. This was true of the many explorers who set off to find new sea routes between Europe and Asia by way of the perilous Northwest and Northeast Passages to the north of Canada and Russia, respectively. Some explorers, like David Livingstone in Africa, were seeking new converts to their religion. Yet others were sent by their rulers to found new colonies and open up new territories for settlement. Often the discoveries made by the explorers were very different from those they expected. For example, Christopher Columbus had no idea that he would find an entirely new continent – he was simply looking for a new route to Asia. But whatever the reasons for their expeditions, the great explorers all needed courage, determination and the will to overcome great difficulties. Very few set out without support and help from people at home. Mounting an expedition has always been expensive. Transport must be provided. Equipment and supplies must be bought. Rulers or their governments have been the greatest supporters of exploration throughout history – from Henry the Navigator, the fifteenth-century Portuguese king who started exploring Africa and the sea routes to the East, to the American and Russian space agencies that in our century have paid for the exploration of space. Some modern explorers have been helped by companies that have sponsored them in return for television and press publicity. Behind most expeditions there have been teams of people – scientists, shipbuilders, storekeepers, suppliers of food and equipment – on whose skills the leaders have depended, and they have shared in the successes and failures of the explorers themselves.

Many of the most successful journeys of discovery were made possible by the advice and assistance of the people already living in those remote areas. Sadly, native peoples, such as the American Indians, did not always benefit from the help they gave to these visitors to their lands.

We must not forget, either, the people who travelled with the famous names you can read about in this book. Few explorers have travelled alone. Some expeditions have included dozens or even hundreds of sailors, porters or guides. The names of most of these people are unknown, but they also deserve to be remembered. They too needed courage to venture out into the unknown, uncertain whether they would ever see their homes and families again. Some did not come back. Others lived through experiences that would haunt them for the rest of their lives. All were true explorers, even if their names are not to be found in books. This book is a tribute to them as well as to their more famous leaders.

Ferdinand Magellan (top left)
Marco Polo (bottom left)
Vostok I (top centre)
Yuri Gagarin's rocket
Nils Nordenskjold (right)

Juan Sebastián del Cano
(c. 1460–1526)

When Ferdinand Magellan (see page 9) was killed on his epic voyage around the world, Juan Sebastián del Cano took over.

Del Cano, an experienced Spanish sailor, captained one of the five ships that set out on Magellan's expedition in 1519, but he had also been one of the leaders of a mutiny on the voyage. Del Cano was lucky to escape with his life.

On Magellan's death, del Cano faced a difficult task. Only 108 were left of 250 men who had set out – too few to crew the remaining three ships, so del Cano decided to burn one. Then they set out for home by way of the Spice Islands. One ship, the *Trinidad*, decided to return eastwards to America. Del Cano finally arrived home with only eighteen men in September 1522, nearly three years after they had set out.

▲ This world map was drawn in the fifteenth century, before del Cano returned from his voyage.

Despite the horrors of his experience with Magellan, Juan Sebastian del Cano set out once again in 1526 on a voyage this time to the Spice Islands. The aim was to return with a valuable cargo of spices, but the expedition was ill-fated – the leader of the expedition died and del Cano took over. Del Cano himself died on the same voyage.

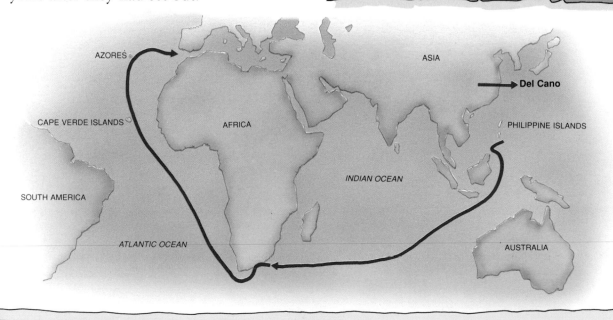

Ferdinand Magellan
(1480-1521)

Death robbed Ferdinand Magellan of the glory of being the first explorer to sail all the way around the world. Born in 1480, in Portugal, he spent years studying navigation before he offered to lead an expedition for the King of Spain to search for a westward route to the Spice Islands of the East Indies. In September 1519, five ships crewed by about 250 men set out.

The westward crossing of the Atlantic to Brazil went smoothly, but then things began to go wrong. One of the ships was wrecked in a storm off the coast of Patagonia. Then several of Magellan's captains plotted against him, and one of the ships turned back. Magellan had one of the conspirators put to death and left two stranded when he set sail again.

The rest sailed on through the narrow channel that divides South America from Tierra del Fuego, the island at its tip. This strait is now named after Magellan. Supplies were short as the remaining three ships sailed across the Pacific. But there was worse to come. When the ships reached the Marianas Islands, the local people attacked them. Magellan was killed in a fight with tribesmen on the island of Mactan in the Philippines. Eventually, one ship, the *Victoria*, captained by Juan Sebastián del Cano (see page 8), returned to Spain in September 1522. The round trip had been completed, but without its leader.

It was Ferdinand Magellan who gave the Pacific Ocean its modern name. (Balboa had called it the 'Great South Sea'.) After sailing through the stormy Straits of Magellan, the expedition found calmer waters, with steady and gentle winds to carry them westwards. This was, Magellan decided, a peaceful, or Pacific, ocean.

◀ This map of 1650 shows the Straits of Magellan, between South America and Tierra del Fuego.

Francis Drake
(c. 1543-1596)

Francis Drake was the first British seaman to sail around the world. In 1577, Queen Elizabeth I appointed him to make a voyage to the southern Pacific, via South America.

He sailed down the west coast of Africa, then across the Atlantic, reaching Brazil in the spring of 1578. Then he sailed southwards, down the coast of South America. Drake discovered the sea passage that separates Tierra del Fuego (at the the southernmost point of South American) from Antarctica and it is now named after him.

To get home to Engand, he sailed the *Golden Hind* up the Pacific coast of South and North America, and then across the Pacific to the Spice Islands and round the Cape of Good Hope. For the Spanish gold he brought back with him, Queen Elizabeth rewarded him with a knighthood .

▼ Drake's fleet is shown arriving at the port of Santo Domingo, on the island of Hispaniola (now the Dominican Republic).

Drake's later career included two famous attacks on the Spanish fleet - or Armada. In the first, he destroyed a large part of the fleet as it assembled in Cadiz harbour. In 1588, he played a major part in the defeat of the Armada in the English Channel when the English Navy sent blazing fireships among the enemy fleet.

Hirkhouf
(c. 2420 BC)

Between 4,000 and 5,000 years ago, Ancient Egypt was at the centre of an empire that stretched westwards along the North African coast and eastwards to the Red Sea and the eastern shores of the Mediterranean. This was a time of peace in Egypt, when the Egyptians sought to expand their empire by trade rather than war.

In about 2420 BC the Pharaoh, or ruler, of Egypt sent one of his princes, Hirkhouf, on three expeditions to explore the neighbouring state of Nubia, to the south of Egypt (part of what is now Sudan). Hirkhouf's mission was to establish trading links with the Nubians.

Teams of slaves and donkeys carried everything the party would need – water, bread, clothes, barley beer, and goods to trade. They built fortresses along their route for shelter from sandstorms and trading posts where goods could be exchanged.

▲ This Phoenician relief shows the types of ship used in northern Africa at the time of Hirkhouf's expeditions along the River Nile.

Hirkhouf brought back precious stones and other minerals from Nubia. He also brought back a pigmy, whom he called a 'Deng', to act as the Pharaoh's court jester and to entertain the Pharaoh's son Pepi. Pepi's letter of thanks was inscribed on the wall of Hirkhouf's tomb at Aswan in Upper Egypt.

▶ A map of Africa and the Mediterranean. Hirkhouf explored lands to the south of Egypt, to set up trade routes.

Hanno
(c. 450 BC)

Hanno came from the ancient North African city of Carthage. This stood on the Mediterranean coast of present-day Tunisia. About 2,500 years ago it was the capital of a rich and powerful state. Its wealth and strength depended on its large fleet of trading ships and huge navy.

▲ The western coast of Africa where Hanno and his crew first explored, 2,500 years ago.

Carthage needed more land for its growing population. Its leaders had been fighting for more than one hundred years for land in Sicily and southern Italy where they could set up new colonies. Hanno decided to find out if there was land to the west, beyond the Straits of Gibraltar, that could be conquered.

Around 460 BC, Hanno sailed through the Straits into the Atlantic and headed south along the African coast. It was a voyage into the unknown. For the first time, the civilizations of the Mediterranean met those of West Africa. At points along the coast, in present-day Senegal and Guinea, Hanno left groups of Carthaginians behind as settlers. He sailed on, following the African coast as it turns east, until he reached the Bight of Benin, where the coast again turns south.

On his return, Hanno wrote a report of his voyage that was inscribed on a tablet in the Phoenician language. A later translation into ancient Greek still exists. It is the earliest first-hand account of an explorer's adventures.

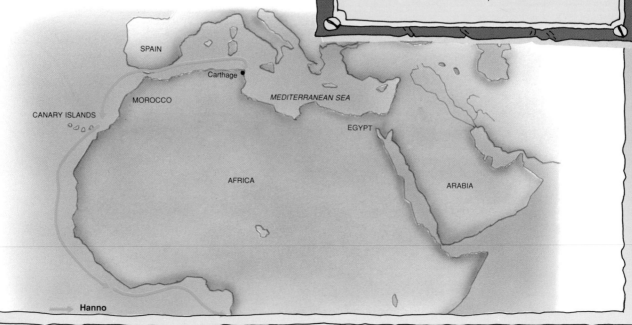

SPAIN

Carthage

MOROCCO

MEDITERRANEAN SEA

CANARY ISLANDS

EGYPT

AFRICA

ARABIA

Hanno

Bartolomeu Dias
(1450–1500)

In 1487 Bartolomeu Dias was chosen by King John II of Portugal to explore the southernmost point of Africa. He became the first European to sail round the Cape of Good Hope

Dias and his crew set out in August 1487 and travelled southwards along the coast of southwest Africa. But they ran into storms that carried them west into the Atlantic Ocean. Out of sight of land, the crews had no idea where they were and were terrified that they might fall off the edge of the world. So when the storms died down, Dias turned back east. They sailed for many days, expecting to reach the coast of Africa, but without success. Dias realized that they must have passed the southern end of Africa. He turned north and eventually landed at Mosselbaai, about 320 kilometres east of what we now know as the Cape of Good Hope.

Dias did not reach India, as he had hoped, because his men refused to go on, but he helped to plan Vasco da Gama's successful voyage in 1497. He advised on the design of the ships and even sailed part of the way with him (see page 51). In 1499 Dias accompanied Pedro Cabral (see page 96) on the voyage to Brazil. However, Dias was drowned later on the same voyage when his ship sank in a storm off the Cape of Good Hope.

The great voyages of exploration made by Dias and other Portuguese and Spanish navigators later in the fifteenth century owed their success, in part, to the design of their boats. These fast boats known as 'caravels' were broad enough to carry sufficient supplies and their sails worked well in different wind conditions.

Mungo Park
(1771-1806)

In 1795 Mungo Park, a young Scottish surgeon, was asked by the African Society (an organization that aimed to find out more about the interior of Africa) to explore the River Niger in West Africa. He travelled inland from the coast of what is now the Gambia. After 900 kilometres, he reached the edge of the Sahara Desert. Here, he was captured by a Moorish chieftain and imprisoned for four months. Escaping with only his horse and a compass, on 21 July 1796 he reached the Niger at Segu in Mali. It was another eleven months before he returned to his base on the coast.

Park undertook his second expedition in 1805. His plan, he wrote to his wife, was to travel down the Niger from Segu

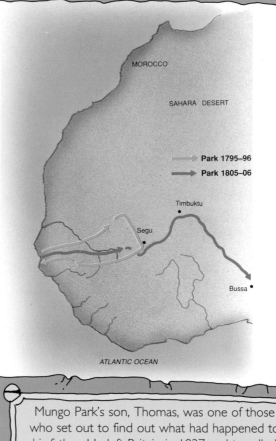

Mungo Park's son, Thomas, was one of those who set out to find out what had happened to his father. He left Britain in 1827 and travelled inland from the West African coast, having heard a rumour that his father was being held prisoner on the Niger. The rumour was false – but Thomas Park never found this out. He died of fever after travelling only a short way.

to the sea. It was the last she ever heard from him. Over twenty years later, a party sent out to investigate Park's disappearance pieced together the story. He had travelled downriver about 1,600 kilometres, reaching the falls at Bussa in present-day Nigeria, when he and his companions were attacked from the shore by Africans. In an attempt to escape, the men jumped into the river and were drowned.

◀ Mungo Park's life ended in a struggle with local people in what is now Nigeria. But it was the waters of the Niger that finally defeated Park and his men as their escape attempt went wrong.

Hugh Clapperton
(1788-1827)

Hugh Clapperton was a Scottish naval officer who twice explored North and West Africa. The first expedition, which aimed to discover whether the River Niger flowed into Lake Chad, started out in 1822. Clapperton, with two companions and guides, travelled south across the Sahara by camel from Tripoli, in what is now Libya. It was a gruelling journey of 2,010 kilometres. They became the first Europeans to see Lake Chad.

Leaving one of the party, Dixon Denham, at Lake Chad, Clapperton and the third member of the party, Walter Oudney, travelled 1,450 kilometres westwards, across what is now Nigeria, to Sokoto. Oudney died on this leg of the journey. Clapperton returned east and he and Denham journeyed back to England in 1825.

Later that year, Clapperton set out again for Africa leading a four-man expedition to find out what had happened to Mungo Park, who had disappeared in 1806 while exploring the Niger (see page 14). Soon after they landed at Badagri, near the present city

▲ Hugh Clapperton, explorer of Africa and the first European to see Lake Chad.

of Lagos in Nigeria, two of the party died of fever. Clapperton and his servant, Richard Lander, who later became a famous explorer in his own right (see page 17) continued to the Bussa Rapids, where Mungo Park had died, and travelled on to Sokoto. Here, Clapperton was imprisoned by hostile Africans and died of fever in April 1827.

The journey across the Sahara Desert is among the greatest challenges a traveller can face. The fierce dry heat, sandstorms and, in Clapperton's day, desert bandits were among the hazards. Temperatures can reach 57 degrees centigrade in the shade by day, while at night they often drop below freezing.

René Auguste Caillié
(1799–1838)

In 1824 a French scientific society offered a prize of 10,000 francs to the first European to visit the town of Timbuktu in present-day Mali, on the edge of the Sahara, and write a report on it. The challenge was taken up by Caillié, an experienced traveller in West Africa and a fluent speaker of Arabic.

Caillié set out eastwards from the coast in 1827, disguised as an Arab traveller. He got close to Timbuktu by joining a number of caravans, but was delayed for five months by fever on the way. He completed the last part of the journey by boat, arriving in Timbuktu on 20 April 1828. His disguise worked, and he was able to spend two weeks in the city undetected as a European traveller. After his stay, Caillié made his way north by caravan to Morocco, where he sailed for France.

Back in France, he was awarded the prize and published a three-volume account of his adventures. In 1838 he died, at the age of 39, from a fever he had caught on his journey.

TANGIER
Fez
MOROCCO
SAHARA DESERT
CAPE VERDE
Timbuktu
SENEGAL
Segu   Djenné
Volta
ATLANTIC OCEAN

▰ ▰ ▶ Caille 1816
⟶ Caille 1827–28

Situated on the southern fringe of the Sahara, Timbuktu has for centuries been the crossroads for caravan trails leading across the Sahara to the West African coast. Many Europeans had tried to travel there, attracted by tales of great palaces and wealthy traders. However, before Caillié, no travellers had returned alive.

▼ In the mid-nineteenth century, about fifty years after Caillé's visit, Timbuktu still had many of its traditional mud-brick houses.

Richard Lemon Lander
(1804-1834)

Richard Lemon Lander began his career in exploration as a servant to Hugh Clapperton (see page 15), travelling out with him to West Africa on his second expedition. Lander began his travels as a merchant's servant when he was only 11 years old. By 1825, he was a very experienced traveller. Lander and Clapperton stayed together throughout the two-year tour and, when Clapperton died, Lander returned home with his journal of the expedition. He arranged for it to be published together with his own story of their adventures.

In 1830 Lander was appointed to lead a British expedition to explore the lower part of the River Niger, which lay in territory unexplored by Europeans. He travelled overland from Badagri, in what is now Nigeria, with his brother John and a group of African guides. Then they worked their way downstream by canoe, mapping the course accurately as they went. They were captured and imprisoned by hostile Africans, but bought their release and continued their journey. They eventually reached the mouth of the Niger in the Gulf of Guinea – the first Europeans to do so.

On his last expedition to the Niger, Richard Lander was attacked by Africans and was badly injured. He died at Fernando Po, an island off the Nigerian coast, on 20 January 1834.

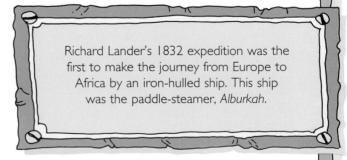

Richard Lander's 1832 expedition was the first to make the journey from Europe to Africa by an iron-hulled ship. This ship was the paddle-steamer, *Alburkah*.

◀ The River Niger threads its way through woods and scrubland to its mouth in Nigeria. Lander passed here in his canoe in 1830.

David Livingstone
(1813-1873)

David Livingstone was a Scottish doctor and missionary who devoted his life to the exploration of central Africa.

He first went to Africa in 1840. Over the next few years he made several expeditions, including a crossing of the Kalahari Desert in 1849 and the discovery of the Victoria Falls, as he named them, on the Zambezi River in 1855. The meticulous notes he made on these journeys enabled the map of Africa to be gradually filled in.

In 1866, Livingstone was back in Africa. He headed an expedition to find the source of the River Nile. His party faced fever, threats from slave-traders, and the theft of food and medical supplies, and eventually set up camp at Ujiji on the shores of Lake Tanganyika.

In 1871, when nothing had been heard of him for some time, the American newspaper, *The New York Herald*, mounted a search under Henry Morton Stanley (see page 22). Stanley found Livingstone at Ujiji in October 1871. The two explorers became firm friends and together made numerous journeys.

Livingstone was strongly against the trade in slaves that was still common in Africa at that time. He had many friends among the African peoples he met. In 1873, after his death, his African servants carried his embalmed body 1,600 kilometres to the coast so that it could be brought back to England. He is buried in Westminster Abbey.

▼ David Livingstone in his ship, the *Ma-Robert*, on the Zambezi River during his expedition of 1855.

Samuel White Baker
(1821-1893)

Samuel White Baker was an experienced British traveller who began to explore Africa at the age of 40. He travelled with his wife Florence, which was most unusual for the time, and they set out to find the source of the River Nile.

▲ A hippopotamus attacks Samuel White Baker's boat during the night at Ismailia, on the River Nile.

In 1861 two British explorers, John Speke and James Grant, (see page 20) were also searching for the source of the Nile. They had started out from East Africa while Samuel and Florence White Baker travelled south from Cairo. The two parties met in Gondokoro, in southern Sudan. The Bakers were disappointed to hear that Speke and Grant had already established that Lake Victoria was a major source of the Nile. But the explorers suggested that there was another great lake to be discovered, so the Bakers pressed on southwards. For a month they toiled up the valley of the Nile, and on 14 March 1864 they sighted a lake. Baker named it Lake Albert after Queen Victoria's husband, the Prince Consort.

Florence, Samuel White Baker's wife, was rescued by her future husband from a Turkish slave-market in Bulgaria in 1859. She had been captured by the Turks at the age of 17 and was about to be sold into a life of slavery, when Baker took pity on her and bought her himself.

▼ Samuel White Baker travelling by bullock in Africa, during a hunting expedition. After he returned from exploring Lake Albert, he became one of the leading hunters of his time.

John Hanning Speke (1827-1864) & Richard Burton (1821-1890)

John Hanning Speke was an officer in the British army who had served in India. In 1857 he set out with Richard Francis Burton to find the source of the westerly branch of the Nile, known as the White Nile.

They set out from Zanzibar, an island off the coast of present-day Tanzania and travelled westwards. They had to make frequent stops due to illness and exhaustion. It was February 1858 before they became the first Europeans to see Lake Tanganyika.

Burton was ill and needed further rest. Leaving his companion at their base at Ujiji, Speke went off on his own. After travelling for three weeks, he discovered Africa's largest lake, which he named Victoria after his queen. Speke was sure that Lake Victoria was one of the main sources of the Nile. Burton, however, disagreed, believing that that Lake Tanganyika was the true source.

In 1860-2 Speke made a further exploration of Lake Victoria, this time with a different companion, James Grant. He found a great river flowing out from the northern shore of the lake. Speke was in no doubt that this was the Nile, but Burton was not convinced.

In 1864, scientists in Britain arranged for Burton and Speke to discuss their views in public. The meeting was arranged in Bath, England, for 15 September. The day before, while out partridge-shooting, Speke was killed by a shot from his own gun.

Richard Francis Burton was one of the most learned travellers of his time. He could speak over thirty eastern languages and translated books from these languages into English, including the *Arabian Nights*. In 1853 he visited the holy Islamic cities of Mecca and Medina, disguised as an Arab.

◀ In the nineteenth century, foreign travellers were often feared and westerners were forbidden to travel in some Arab countries. This was why Burton, and other explorers, often disguised themselves in local dress when journeying abroad.

Gustav Nachtigal

(1834-1885)

In 1863, King Frederick III of Prussia appointed Nachtigal, a German army surgeon who had been on a number of expeditions to Africa, to travel to Bornu, near Lake Chad. Bornu was then an independent Muslim state, and Frederick III wanted to open up trading and military links.

Nachtigal travelled south from Tripoli in Libya, across the dry wastes of the Sahara in stages from oasis to oasis and through the remote Tibesti Mountains.

Eventually he reached Bornu and was able to deliver King Frederick III's messages to the Sultan. Nachtigal made several expeditions north of Lake Chad, then he went eastwards across the southern Sahara and north to Cairo. In all, the expedition took him five years.

On his return to Germany, Nachtigal wrote the first detailed description of the southeastern Sahara.

▲ Nachtigal departs from Tripoli on his expedition to Bornu. With him are companions Gerhard Rohls and Mohammed el Gatruni.

The Tibesti Mountains were so inaccessible to outsiders that, after Nachtigal's exploration, no European visited them for another forty-five years. In 1915, the area was mapped by a British military expedition. Since 1960 the mountains have been part of the Republic of Chad.

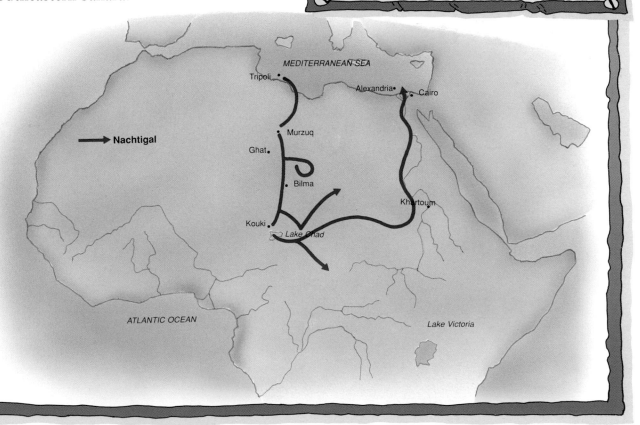

Henry Morton Stanley
(1841-1904)

Stanley's real name was John Rowlands. He was born in Wales, but ran away to sea when he was 15 years old and ended up in the United States. He was adopted by a wealthy businessman, John Morton Stanley, whose name he later took. During the American Civil War, Stanley fought for the South. He later became a journalist.

In 1869 the *New York Herald*, the newspaper for which Stanley worked, sent him to Africa to search for David Livingstone, the British explorer who had disappeared there (see page 18). On the way, Stanley stopped off in Egypt to report the opening of the Suez Canal.

In March 1871 Stanley set off from Zanzibar, an island off the coast of present-day Tanzania, to look for Livingstone. Travelling west, he eventually found Livingstone on 10 November, 1871 at Ujiji, on the shores of Lake Tanganyika.

Stanley made three more journeys in Africa. In 1874-7 he travelled westwards from Lake Tanganyika along the Lualaba River. This joins the huge Congo River (now the Zaire River) down which he journeyed to the sea. His next expedition in 1879-84 was for King Leopold II of Belgium. Stanley established the Congo Free State in the jungle of central Africa. His final African adventure in 1887-9 was in the service of Emin Pasha of Sudan.

▲ This picture shows Stanley against the background of his many exploits in Africa. It was painted in the 1890s, after the explorer had retired.

Stanley's meeting with Livingstone began with four of the most famous words in the history of exploration. Stanley stepped forward into a clearing where Livingstone was sitting, stretched out his hand, and said, 'Doctor Livingstone, I presume?'

Pierre Savorgnan de Brazza
(1852-1905)

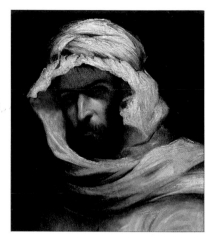

In around 1870, European countries began to look towards Africa for land to add to their empires, and what became known as 'the scramble for Africa' began. France was beaten by Prussia in the war of 1870-71, and was particularly keen to take territories in Africa to get back its position as a world power.

In 1875, Pierre de Brazza, an officer in the French navy, offered to explore the region of Gabon in west central Africa. The expedition took three years.

He travelled by boat from the west African coast up the Ogooué River. Brazza thought that this would join the Congo (now Zaire) River, but he failed to find it.

In 1880 he was sent back to explore further and colonize land in the Congo region. On this expedition he founded the town of Brazzaville, now the capital of the Congo. Brazza persuaded many African tribal chiefs to sign treaties agreeing to place their lands under French protection. In his travels he met Henry Morton Stanley (see page 22), who was on a similar mission for the Belgian government. They were carving up the Congo region between them, taking payment for the treaties they signed.

In 1883 Brazza became governor of the French colony in the Congo, a post he held until 1898.

The colony founded by Brazza in the Congo stayed in French possession until 1960, when it became independent. It is now known as the People's Republic of the Congo.

The land that Stanley took became known as the Belgian Congo. In 1960, with independence, it became the Democratic Republic of the Congo. In 1971 its name was changed to Zaire.

◀ Some of the African chiefs met by Brazza on his travels are shown in this engraving of the 1880s.

Mary Kingsley
(1862-1900)

Mary Kingsley grew up in London with an ambition to travel, having read many travel books in her father's library. She was unable to do anything about it for some years, as both her parents became invalids and she had to stay at home to care for them. When they died, she lost little time in planning her first journey to West Africa. She spent five months in 1893-4 travelling near the Congo River, observing African customs.

Her second journey, starting in December 1894, was even more adventurous. She landed on the coast of Gabon and travelled up the Ogooué River by canoe.

Mary Kingsley seems to have been completely without fear. She moved freely among the cannibal Fang people of the region and traded with them by barter. Her belief that Europeans need not fear Africans if they showed them kindness was proved by her own experiences. After many months of hard travel, which included climbing the 4,195-metre Great Cameroon Mountain by a route not attempted before, Mary Kingsley returned to London in October 1895.

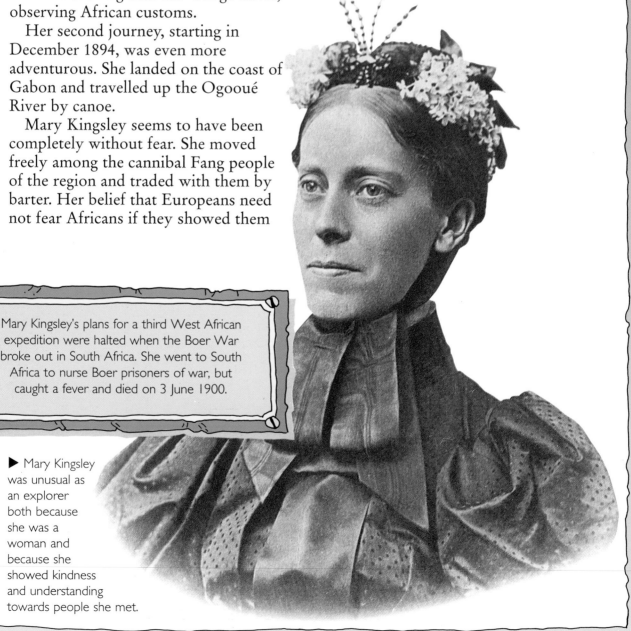

Mary Kingsley's plans for a third West African expedition were halted when the Boer War broke out in South Africa. She went to South Africa to nurse Boer prisoners of war, but caught a fever and died on 3 June 1900.

▶ Mary Kingsley was unusual as an explorer both because she was a woman and because she showed kindness and understanding towards people she met.

James Clark Ross
(1800–1862)

James Clark Ross, the nephew of John Ross (see page 35), was an experienced Arctic sailor who had travelled with his uncle to the Arctic and reached the magnetic North Pole. He had expert knowledge of the Earth's magnetic field, so was chosen to lead an expedition which set out in 1839 to find the magnetic South Pole. His ships, the *Erebus* and the *Terror*, were specially strengthened to withstand the ice.

On 5 January 1841, Ross's ships forced their way into the Antarctic ice south of New Zealand. They rammed a passage through the ice into the open sea, and became the first ships to pass through the ice pack. The sea was later named after Ross.

On his second expedition, Ross and his team reached further south than ever before, but still failed to reach the Pole.

In 1848-9 James Clark Ross led one of the many expeditions sent to the Arctic to discover what had become of Sir John Franklin and his men (see page 36). With two new ships, he searched the west coast of Greenland, but became trapped in Lancaster Sound by the ice for the winter. Although he was close to Franklin's route, Ross discovered no sign of him.

▼ Ross's two ships, the *Erebus* and the *Terror*, had to withstand thick ice and raging storms.

Roald Amundsen
(1872-1928)

Roald Amundsen was a Norwegian who achieved two 'firsts' in the history of exploration. He was the first to sail the Northwest Passage and the first to reach the South Pole.

His expedition to find the Northwest Passage began in June 1903. The party camped for two winters on King William Island, well inside the Arctic Circle, and spent the following winter on Mackenzie Island. They completed the voyage to the Pacific in September 1906.

Amundsen left Norway for the South Pole, in Nansen's ship the *Fram* (see page 40), in November 1910. From his base on the eastern end of the Ross Ice Shelf, he made the final assault on the South Pole on 20 October 1911, ahead of his British rival Captain Scott (see page 27). With four companions on dog-sledges, he reached the Pole on 14 December 1911.

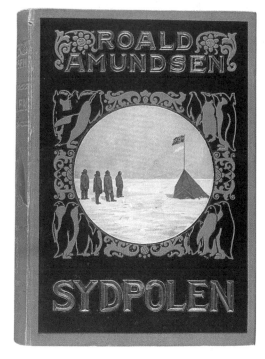

▲ When he returned, Amundsen wrote a book describing his journey. The cover is decorated with a photograph of the team at the South Pole itself.

Roald Amundsen became one of the first two explorers to fly over the North Pole. In 1926, he and the Italian explorer Umberto Nobile circled the Pole twice in an airship. Two years later Amundsen disappeared while searching for Nobile, whose airship had crashed on another flight over the North Pole

▼ Amundsen and his men shelter in their winter quarters in Antarctica. This was where they mended their equipment, rested, and prepared for their assault on the South Pole.

Robert Falcon Scott
(1868-1912)

Robert Falcon Scott was a British naval officer who failed in his ambition to be the first man to reach the South Pole. His rival Roald Amundsen (see page 26) arrived there just over a month earlier.

In June 1910, Scott set out in the *Terra Nova*. On the way, he learned that Amundsen, too, was going to the Pole.

Scott's party left their base camp for the Pole on 1 November 1911. Blizzards made the going difficult, so on 3 January 1912, Scott decided to go on with only four companions, Edward Wilson, Lawrence Oates, Henry Bowers and Edgar Evans. On 17 January they reached the South Pole. But there was already Amundsen's Norwegian flag fluttering there. Deeply disappointed, the four began their return journey. Evans was injured in a fall and died.

Oates had severe frostbite, and rather than hold up the others he walked out into a blizzard and was never seen again. The three remaining men made a camp to shelter from the weather, but on 29 March, all three died. They were only a few kilometres from their base camp.

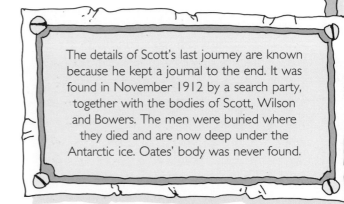

The details of Scott's last journey are known because he kept a journal to the end. It was found in November 1912 by a search party, together with the bodies of Scott, Wilson and Bowers. The men were buried where they died and are now deep under the Antarctic ice. Oates' body was never found.

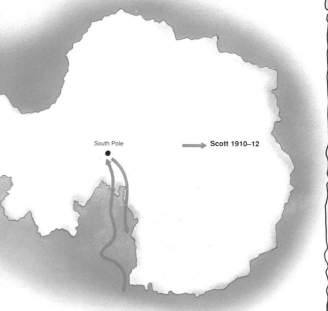

◀ This photograph of Scott was taken by another member of the British Antarctic Expedition, Herbert Ponting. Soon afterwards, Ponting would be one of those who would return to base, leaving Scott and his four companions to push on to the Pole.

South Pole

Scott 1910–12

Douglas Mawson
(1882-1958)

Douglas Mawson was born in England, but emigrated to Australia as a boy. He first went to the Antarctic with a British party in 1907. In 1911, he returned as leader of an Australian scientific expedition.

After a winter at base camp, the expedition split up into small groups. Mawson set out with two others, Mertz and Ninnis. Mawson led the way, with Ninnis at the rear, with a dog-sledge carrying their supplies. Suddenly Ninnis, his sledge, and his team of dogs disappeared. They had fallen into a deep crevasse. There was no hope of rescuing him, or of going on with no supplies, so Mawson and Mertz were forced to turn back.

They were 480 kilometres from base, with little food and only one sleeping-bag. They had to kill and eat the remaining dogs. After Mertz fell ill and died, Mawson travelled alone for 160 kilometres, only to find that his support ship had left. He had to spend a second winter at base before he was rescued.

▲ The dramatic landscape of Antarctica, through which Mawson and his team travelled. Crevasses – deep cracks in the ice – are a great hazard to climbers and walkers; Mawson's expedition was halted because a team member fell into one.

Douglas Mawson's ordeal earned him a knighthood when he returned to Australia in 1914. His experiences did not deter him from further exploration in the Antarctic. He headed a joint Australian, British and New Zealand research expedition between 1929 and 1931.

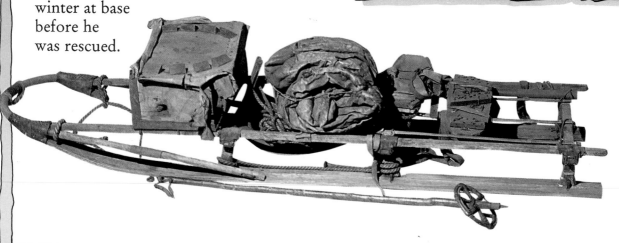

Vivian Fuchs
(born 1908)

Vivian Fuchs was the leader of the first expedition to complete a crossing of the Antarctic. As a British geologist, he had spent three years there setting up scientific research stations. He was marooned for a year by bad weather on Graham Land on the Antarctic Peninsula. He spent this time planning his polar crossing.

Fuchs set out from Shackleton Base, on the coast of the Weddell Sea, on 24 November 1957. His team of ten men was equipped with six tracked vehicles, known as 'sno-cats', which towed sledges carrying supplies. Even with such modern equipment, the crossing was challenging. There were deep crevasses crossed by snow bridges that were not always strong enough to take the weight of the sno-cats. The team had to repair the vehicles in temperatures down to minus 51 degrees centigrade. The party reached the South Pole on 19 January 1958. There, they met another expedition led by the New Zealand conqueror of Mount Everest, Sir Edmund Hillary. Fuchs' party continued, using bases that had been set up by Hillary, and on 2 March 1958 they reached Scott Base, Victoria Land.

Vivian Fuchs' expedition was launched to celebrate the United Nations' International Geophysical Year, 1957-8. International scientific co-operation in the Antarctic led to the Antarctic Treaty, forbidding military activity, nuclear explosions and the dumping of radioactive waste in the region.

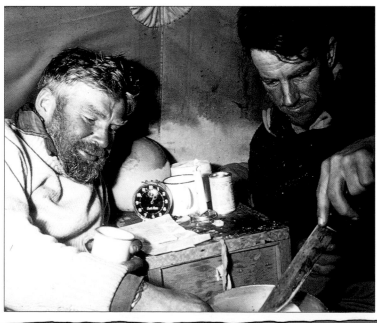

▶ Vivian Fuchs and Edmund Hillary eat a meal in their tent during the Trans-Antarctic Expedition.

Erik the Red
(c.950-c.1003)

Erik the Red was a Viking sailor, born in Norway. He discovered Greenland and founded a Viking settlement there. In AD 981 he set out from Iceland to explore Greenland, sailing round the coast from east to west until he found an ice-free place to land. After spending three years there, Erik returned to Iceland in 985 to collect a party of families who would settle in Greenland and establish a Viking colony. He gave the country the name 'Greenland' to make it sound more attractive to the settlers. The conditions there must have shocked them when they arrived.

In 986 Erik the Red led an expedition of twenty-five ships, of which only fourteen, containing about 500 people, arrived in Greenland. They founded the settlement of Brattahlid, near the southwestern tip of the country, where the climate is warmest. The settlers earned their living by fishing and trapping.

The Viking settlements in Greenland lasted for about 500 years and then disappeared. The last ship to trade between Norway and Greenland sailed in 1410. Possibly the families on Greenland were struck by disease, or it may be that they found it easier to mix and trade with the Inuit people further north.

▶ With their single sails billowing in the strong northern winds, the Vikings' ships approach the icy coast of Greenland.

Richard Chancellor
(died 1556)

Richard Chancellor took part in two expeditions to find a Northeast Passage to China organized by Sebastian Cabot (see page 97). He was second-in-command of the first voyage, which set off in May 1553, under the command of Sir Hugh Willoughby. Neither knew much about conditions in the Arctic, and only Chancellor's ship survived.

Chancellor sailed around the north of Norway and Lapland until he reached Arkhangel'sk in northern Russia. This was the land of the notorious Ivan the Terrible, the Tsar of Muscovy. As they could not leave, because winter was closing in, Chancellor set out on the 1,300-kilometre journey to Moscow to make a treaty with Ivan.

Chancellor was received kindly by the Tsar, who agreed to allow English ships to trade at the northern Russian ports.

▲ Pack ice and snowy, mountainous coasts – these were the conditions that met Chancellor on his voyage to find the Northeast Passage. The seas were treacherous and the inland conditons even worse.

◄ To his surprise, Chancellor was well received by the Tsar when he got to Moscow. But when he made a return trip in 1556 he met disaster. His ship was wrecked and Chancellor was drowned.

The disappearance of Sir Hugh Willoughby, the commander of Chancellor's 1553 voyage, remained a mystery until the following year. Separated from Chancellor, Sir Hugh had sailed on and eventually reached Lapland where he decided to spend the winter. His frozen body and those of his crew were found by a Russian fisherman in the spring of 1554.

Martin Frobisher
(c. 1535-1594)

Martin Frobisher was the first English navigator to explore the Arctic Ocean. As a young man he spent many years as a 'privateer'. This is a polite way of describing the English pirates who attacked the Spanish ships carrying treasure from the New World, with the secret support of Queen Elizabeth I.

In 1576, Frobisher set out with three ships to search for the Northwest Passage. Almost at once, disaster struck. The smallest of the three ships sank in the Atlantic waves. Another was separated from Frobisher's in a storm and returned to port. This left Frobisher's own ship, the *Gabriel*, to continue alone.

After exploring Baffin Island, off Canada's northeast coast, Frobisher returned home, bringing with him samples of a black rock that he thought might contain gold. Excited by this, Queen Elizabeth I invested in a second and third expedition. These brought back about 1,500 tons of the black rock, but it turned out to be worthless.

The fruitless search for gold took over from Frobisher's attempt to find the Northwest Passage, but his descriptions of the Arctic shore and the terrible sailing conditions to be found there inspired later explorers to take up the challenge.

After his return from the Arctic, Frobisher continued his seafaring life and served under the command of Francis Drake (see page 10). He was later knighted for his part in the defeat of the Spanish Armada in 1588.

As well as the worthless black rock, Frobisher brought back from his first voyage 'a strange man of Cathay' - an Inuit (Eskimo) prisoner who had been captured on Baffin Island. The Inuit's Asian appearance convinced Frobisher that he was near to China. He was as wrong about that as he was about the value of the black rock.

▶ On his second expedition to Baffin Island, Frobisher fought with the locals, who tried to defend themselves with bows and arrows.

William Barents
(c. 1550-1597)

The Dutch were a nation of sailors and traders and were keen to find the Northeast Passage from Europe to Asia. William Barents made three attempts – in 1594, 1595 and 1596. On the first two voyages he was driven back by icy conditions. On the third, he discovered the island of Spitsbergen, and a nearby sea was named after him. But he became trapped on the island of Novaya Zemlya when ice crushed his ship. So Barents and his crew built a wooden shack and dug in for the winter.

The hut's central fire could not keep the Arctic cold away. The clothes froze on the men's backs. They managed to kill polar bears and walruses for meat, but their supplies ran short. Two men died, and Barents became very weak.

For three months, the explorers did not see the sun. Then spring came, and they decided to make their escape in two of the ship's open boats that they had saved from the wreck. On 13 June 1597,

the fourteen survivors set out across a sea of ice. 'Every minute of every hour we saw death before our eyes', one of the crew wrote later. Barents died on the voyage home.

▲ Barents and his men managed to build a large wooden hut on Novaya Zemlya, but even this was not enough to protect them from the bitter cold.

In the 1870s, 282 years after Barents' death, Norwegian fishermen discovered his hut on Novaya Zemlya. It had been damaged by Arctic storms but it still contained pots and pans, musical instruments and a clock. Part of Barents' journal was also found, describing the terrible conditions that the explorers lived through that winter.

Vitus Jonassen Bering
(1681–1741)

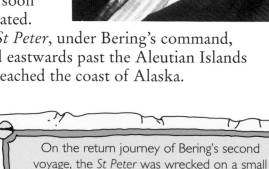

Vitus Jonassen Bering was a Danish sailor who served in the Russian navy. In 1724 Peter the Great, the Tsar of Russia, decided that the eastern coast of his empire must be explored, and Bering was put in charge. The plan was find out whether the northern parts of Asia and America were joined.

Bering made two journeys. The first, partly by sea and partly overland, began in 1725. The land sections took Bering across mountains and through swamps to Kamchatka, a peninsular to the east of Siberia where they set up their base. Here, two ships were built and Bering set out northwards up the coast. After weeks of sailing through thick fog, Bering turned back without finding the answer to the Tsar's question. He was not to know that the fog had prevented him from seeing that he had sailed through the channel between Siberia and Alaska – the Bering Strait.

Bering's second voyage

took eight years to organize but eventually two ships set sail in June 1741. The two ships were soon separated. The *St Peter*, under Bering's command, sailed eastwards past the Aleutian Islands and reached the coast of Alaska.

On the return journey of Bering's second voyage, the *St Peter* was wrecked on a small island off Kamchatka in icy waters. Food supplies ran short and many of the crew perished. Bering himself died from scurvy in December. The following year the survivors managed to rebuild the ship from the wreckage and returned to port.

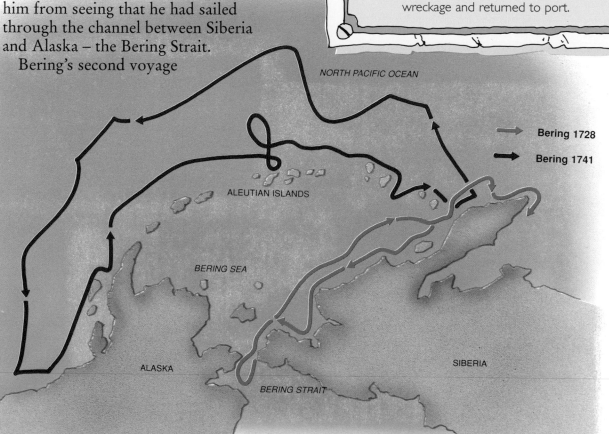

NORTH PACIFIC OCEAN

→ Bering 1728

→ Bering 1741

ALEUTIAN ISLANDS

BERING SEA

ALASKA

BERING STRAIT

SIBERIA

John Ross
(1777-1856)

Rear-Admiral Sir John Ross was a Scottish naval officer who made two voyages to the Arctic in search of the Northwest Passage. His first expedition in 1818 failed, but in 1829 Ross set out again, in command of a paddle-steamer, the *Victory* – the first time such a craft had been used in Arctic exploration. The engine proved unsatisfactory and, when he reached the Arctic, Ross dumped it and the fuel on the ice and continued under sail. For three winters the ship was locked in by ice on the Boothia Peninsula west of Baffin Island. Ross bought dog teams from the local Inuit people and made two long journeys over the ice on dog-sledges. On one of these expeditions, a team that included his nephew James Clark Ross (see page 25) reached the magnetic North Pole.

Rather than face a fourth winter in the Arctic, the expedition abandoned the *Victory* and set out overland for home. When he reached Britain, Ross was rewarded with a knighthood.

In old age, Sir John Ross was again called on to make an Arctic voyage – this time to search for the lost explorer John Franklin (see page 36). The expedition was funded by the Hudson's Bay Company. The year was 1850, and Ross was then 73 years old, but he could not resist the temptation to sail to the Arctic again. However, he found no trace of Franklin.

▼ For crossing the ice, Ross realized that the local form of transport was the best. He bartered with the Inuit people to buy teams of dogs and sledges.

John Franklin
(1786–1847)

What happened to Sir John Franklin and his 1845 expedition to find the Northwest Passage remained a mystery for fourteen years.

Franklin, a 59-year-old rear-admiral of the British navy and an experienced Arctic explorer, sailed with two ships and 120 men in May 1845. His ships, the *Erebus* and the *Terror*, had new steam engines and propellers, and enough supplies on board for three years. Franklin's ships were sighted in Baffin Bay two months later, but never again. Forty expeditions, including one led by Sir John Ross (see page 35) were sent to search for them in the years following their disappearance. But the mystery was not solved until 1859.

A naval expedition, under Leopold McClintock, found skeletons and part of a journal at Cape Felix on King William Island, well inside the Arctic Circle. Franklin's two ships had been trapped in the ice in September 1845. Unable to

free themselves the next summer, they had to endure another winter on board. Franklin died in June 1847. Finally, the remaining members of the expedition set out overland, laden with supplies. It was a fatal decision. Cold, disease and starvation attacked the party. A trail of bodies and belongings was found strung out for miles across the frozen wastes.

Despite its tragic end, Franklin's expedition and the later rescue missions provided a wealth of valuable information about the area. When Roald Amundsen finally sailed the Northwest Passage in 1905, the discovery was dedicated to Franklin.

Food poisoning is thought to have been one of the causes of death among Franklin's men, and possibly of Franklin himself. The expedition's supplies included quantities of canned beef. One theory is that the cans were faulty and that the beef had gone bad.

◀ The British government offered large rewards to anyone who could rescue Franklin or find his ships.

William Edward Parry
(1790-1855)

William Parry acted as second-in-command to John Ross (see page 35) and later led his own expeditions to find the Northwest Passage (the sea route from the Atlantic Ocean along the northern coast of Canada to the Pacific).

His first expedition set out in 1819. Travelling west from Greenland, he sailed over half way to the Pacific and reached Melville Island in 1820. This was further than any expedition had travelled before. Although he had failed to find the Northwest Passage, he made valuable maps of the Arctic coastline.

In June 1827 he set off to find the North Pole. He journeyed from Spitsbergen, an island to the north of Norway, in boats fitted with steel runners so that they could be dragged along the ice like sledges. After travelling north for about four weeks, they were still 800 kilometres from the North Pole. Parry realized that the ice floes on which they were walking were drifting south on the ocean currents. Parry decided to return to base. The expedition had succeeded in travelling nearer to the North Pole than anyone before. This record was not to be broken for another fifty years.

▲ Parry's crew pull their equipment across the ice. They have rigged sails on their sledges, so that the strong wind will help to push them along.

William Parry tried to occupy his crew while they wintered in the Arctic. He organized daily exercise sessions, readings and sing-songs. The men performed a play every two weeks, and they even produced their own newspaper.

▶ Parry kept a journal of his second voyage. It was illustrated by his second-in-command Captain Lyons. This drawing shows local Inuit people.

Nils Nordenskjöld
(1832-1901)

Nils Nordenskjöld was a Finnish-born scientist who made a number of Arctic explorations after he moved to Sweden. In the most famous of these, in 1878-9, he succeeded in sailing the Northeast Passage, which links the Atlantic and Pacific oceans.

The expedition sailed in July 1878 from Tromsø in Norway aboard the *Vega*. This ship had both steam engines and sails. It carried supplies for two years. By September the *Vega* was sailing through thick fog and snowstorms, and because the waters were uncharted a launch had to go ahead to measure the depth. Eventually pack ice made it impossible to go on. Nordenskjöld decided to spend the winter in the ice carrying out scientific research. Ten months later, when the *Vega* was able to continue its voyage, Nordenskjöld found that the Bering Strait and the Pacific were only two days' sailing away. The search for the Northeast Passage was over.

Although Nordenskjöld had succeeded in the centuries-old quest for the Northeast Passage, it was many years before it could be used for trading because the ships at that time were not suitable. It was not until 1915 that a second voyage along the route was made by a Russian ice-breaker. Today, it is regularly used by ships specially built to cope with the icy conditions.

▼ Nordenskjöld battling with the ferocious seas as he attempts to land on the northern coast of Russia.

Robert Edwin Peary
(1856-1920)

In 1909 Robert Peary, a United States naval officer, led the first expedition to reach the North Pole.

He had been preparing for this feat for many years. He made his first polar journey in 1886, and had returned many times. He spent four years in the Arctic making friends with the Inuit and gaining their support for his plan. Peary learned valuable techniques for survival in the Arctic from them.

In 1905 he made his first attempt on the Pole, but had to turn back when supplies ran short. At last, in 1908, Peary set out on what was to prove his successful expedition. On the way he heard that another American, Dr Frederick Cook, was on a similar quest, but with a much smaller team.

Learning from the mistakes of the previous trip, Peary laid out lines of supply across the ice, with food stores at suitable intervals. With about 640

▲ At the foot of this glacier icebergs are frozen into the sea. It is across a landscape like this that Peary and his men made their journey to the North Pole.

kilometres to go to their destination, Peary's party left their ship, the *Roosevelt*, on the last day of February 1909 and took to sledges drawn by dogs. Peary, his companion Matthew Henson and four Inuit took advantage of a spell of fine weather and made a final dash and reached the Pole on 6 April.

Dr Frederick Cook later claimed to have reached the North Pole a year earlier than Peary, and the two men quarrelled bitterly in public. After scientific investigations, Peary's claim was upheld, but he remained bitter about Cook for the rest of his life.

Fridtjof Nansen
(1861-1930)

The Norwegian explorer Fridtjof Nansen is remembered for two achievements in the Arctic. He made the first east-to-west crossing of Greenland, and attempted a spectacular expedition to the North Pole.

Nansen's believed that Arctic currents flowed from the Siberian coast towards the North Pole. Nansen's plan was to let his ship freeze into the Siberian ice and then drift with the current. He had a ship, the *Fram*, specially designed to resist the crushing pressure of the ice. This ship was later used on Amundsen's expedition to the South Pole (see page 26). Nansen set out in June 1893, but it soon became clear that his plan would not work. So he and a companion decided to press on to the Pole on foot; they got within 400 kilometres of their target, closer than anyone previously.

▲ Nansen hoped to get to the Pole by using his knowledge of the Arctic currents to drift with the ice. When this failed, he quickly saw the importance of dogs as a way of crossing the Arctic wastes.

▼ Nansen's ship the *Fram* was specially built for polar exploration. It had a strong hull to resist ice pressure and warm quarters for the expedition leader and his crew.

Tall, active and very fit, with the looks of a Viking, Nansen became a national hero after his Arctic adventures. He became a national and international statesman, and in 1922, won the Nobel Peace Prize for his work in relieving suffering after the Russian Revolution.

Donald MacMillan
(1874-1970)

Donald MacMillan was an American explorer. After studying at Harvard University and spending some years as a teacher, he first travelled to the Arctic in 1908 with Robert Peary's successful expedition to the North Pole (see page 39). This experience was to shape Donald MacMillan's life for the next thirty years.

In 1913 he led his own expedition to Ellesmere Island and Axel Heiberg Island, which lie across the Arctic Circle to the west of Greenland. The purpose of the journey was to find 'Crocker Land', which earlier explorers claimed was north of Axel Heiberg Island. MacMillan was able to report that 'Crocker Land' did not exist but his party carried out a full coastal survey of Ellesmere Island before sailing for home.

MacMillan's later expeditions - of which there were over thirty - included journeys to Labrador, Baffin Island, Greenland and the North Pole. He studied the lives of the Inuit people and discovered coal and fossilized trees inside the Arctic Circle, proving that the climate had been warmer there in prehistoric times.

▲ MacMillan was a keen observer of Arctic people and wildlife. One of the animals he often saw was the Arctic fox, with its thick white fur.

During World War II, Donald MacMillan used his extensive knowledge of the Arctic to advise the United States Navy on secret defence work in the region.

Walter Herbert
(born 1934)

Walter ('Wally') Herbert is a British surveyor who made the first surface crossing of the Arctic in 1968. He had already taken part in an expedition to the South Pole and spent five years exploring northern Greenland.

Herbert's British Trans-Arctic Expedition set out on 21 February 1968. Their plan was to drift part of the way on ice-floes carried by Arctic currents, and travel the rest of the way by sledge.

They arrived at the starting point, to discover that it was in the wrong place to catch the currents. They moved on, but one of the team fell, and they had to return to base to winter there. Finally, on 24 February 1969, they set off again. Early in April, they reached the North Pole, and nearly ten weeks later they arrived on Sptisbergen, an island to the north of Norway. Their journey of 5,820 kilometres had taken them 476 days, and was the longest continuous sledge journey in history.

▲ When travelling around snowy northwestern Greenland, Wally Herbert kept warm with clothes of animal skins, just like the local people.

When Walter Herbert reached what he thought was the North Pole, he sent a radio message to Queen Elizabeth II. He then discovered that he had miscalculated and had several miles still to travel. He had to hurry on to make sure that he was at the Pole by the time the Queen received his message.

BARENT SEA

EUROPE

ARCTIC OCEAN

SPITSBERGEN

BERING STRAIT

North Pole

Herbert

ALASKA

GREENLAND

Naomi Uemura
(1942-1984)

Naomi Uemura was a Japanese explorer whose interest in exploration began when he took up mountaineering. He had a spectacular career as a climber. When he succeeded in climbing Mount Everest in 1970, he became the first person to climb the highest mountain on each of the world's five continents.

In 1977 Uemura travelled to the Canadian Arctic and spent a year living with the Inuit people. He made several long journeys with them by dog sledge, including 12,000 kilometres from Greenland to Alaska, and 725 kilometres on his own by dog-sledge from Ellesmere Island to the North Pole.

Uemura had planned to make a solo crossing of the Antarctic in 1982 but the the Falklands War prevented him. He died in 1984 while climbing Mount McKinley in Alaska. He is known to have reached the top but apparently fell during the descent. Despite searches, his body has never been found.

▲ This abandoned hut at Etah shows the cramped conditions of the base camp a team of mountaineers build before making an attempt on a major peak. Its thick walls give shelter from the freezing wind.

▼ Teams of dogs provided the power for Uemura's sledges as he trekked across Greenland. The men could take turns riding and guiding the dogs.

After his successful climb of Mount Everest in 1970, Naomi Uemura made four later attempts, all of which failed. In 1971 he made two attempts to climb the mountain in winter, and tried again with a Japanese team in 1981.

Chang Ch'ien
(died 114 BC)

In the second century BC the Chinese Empire was troubled by raids by Hun tribes from the mountains to the north and west. They attacked Chinese farmers, stole their cattle, and tried to stir up opposition to Chinese rule.

In 138 BC the Emperor, Wu Ti, sent Chang Ch'ien to the province of Bactria – now part of northern Afghanistan. His mission was to help the people of the region to stand up to the invaders. Chang Ch'ien was captured and held prisoner by the Huns for twelve years, but after his release he set out again to explore the lands to the west of China.

His travels took him through Afghanistan as far as Samarkand in what is now the Uzbek Republic. No one had ever travelled so far west from China. So Chang Ch'ien took back to the Emperor the first news that had been heard in China about India, the Middle East and the countries of Europe.

▲ Much of Afghanistan is mountainous, and these mountains created a barrier between China and the West. Chang Chi'en was the first to travel across this country, although many Chinese traders would follow him in years to come.

Traders from China were later to carry silk and jade along the route that Chang Ch'ien travelled across the mountains to the northwest of China and through the Gobi Desert. This later became known as the 'Great Silk Road'.

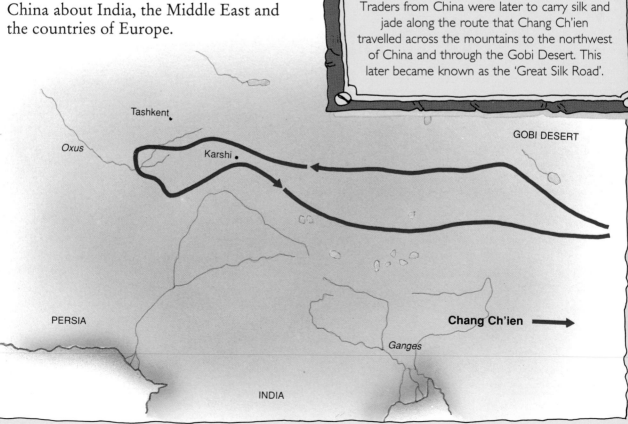

Tashkent

Oxus

Karshi

GOBI DESERT

PERSIA

Chang Ch'ien ➡

Ganges

INDIA

Hsuan Tsang
(c. 600-664)

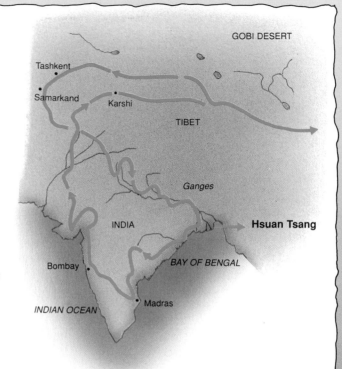

Hsuan Tsang was a Buddhist monk who travelled to India, the home of Buddhism, to find out more about his religion. He set out from China on a journey that was to last sixteen years and take him 64,000 kilometres through Afghanistan, Kashmir and northern India. His journey was kept secret as the Emperor would not allow travel from China to the outside world.

Hsuan Tsang travelled to the edge of the Gobi Desert in central Asia, eastwards as far as Samarkand, and then turned south to cross the mountains of the Hindu Kush into India. In India, he was welcomed as a Buddhist scholar.

When Hsuan Tsang returned to China, the Emperor ordered him to write an account of his travels, which took up most of the rest of his life.

▼ When Hsuan Tsang left behind the peaks of China, he did not realize he was starting a journey that many of his companions would not complete.

Hsuan Tsang's journey took him close to death many times. There was danger from bad weather and high mountains. Hsuan Tsang was almost killed by arrows as he drank from a spring and later, when he was imprisoned in the kingdom of Taxila in northern India, he almost starved to death in order to escape.

Suleyman the Merchant
(c. 850)

The Abbasid Caliphate was an Arabian empire that covered the eastern half of North Africa and stretched across southern Asia as far as India in the ninth century AD. At this time Suleyman, an Abbasid traveller, made a bold journey into India and beyond.

Suleyman began his journey at Siraf, a port on the Persian Gulf, in what is now Iran. His aim was to make contact with Muslim traders in the ports of southeast Asia. He sailed down the Gulf and across the Arabian Sea to Kerala in southern India. Few sailors in those days ventured out into the open sea, beyond the sight of land. However, when Suleyman rounded the southern tip of India, he headed due west across the Indian Ocean close to the Equator. He sailed on to what is now Malaysia. The last leg of his journey took him as far as Canton (now called Guangzhou) in southern China. It was an amazing voyage as he had only very primitive means of navigation.

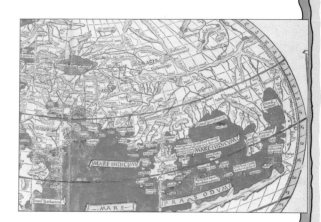

Suleyman wrote a book entitled *Reports in India and China* about his travels. Many people at the time thought that he had invented his descriptions of the places he had visited. But one hundred years later another Abbasid traveller followed the same route and confirmed what Suleyman had written.

▶ Suleyman was also known as the Merchant of Basrah; he traded with the people he met as he travelled.

John of Pian de Carpini
(c. 1180–1253)

Eight hundred years ago, Mongol tribes conquered most of Asia and began to threaten Europe. In 1245, Pope Innocent IV sent a peace mission from Europe to the Mongol capital of Karakorum.

John of Pian de Carpini, a Franciscan monk, was put in charge. He was well into his sixties, and an unlikely choice for such a dangerous journey. The party set out on Easter Day 1245.

Towards the end of the journey, the explorers became very ill. They had only a kind of porridge to eat, and melted snow for drinking water. At last, on 22 July 1245, they arrived at Karakorum.

John Carpini had to wait several months for a meeting with the Mongol ruler, Great Khan Guyuk. It was not until November that the party could leave for home and winter was closing in. Often, the monks had to clear snow from the ground before they could rest for the night. Sometimes, they had to make their beds on the frozen snow.

They arrived home in the summer of 1247 and although Carpini failed to gain the support of the Great Khan for Christianity, his mission provided much valuable information about the vast unknown lands of central Asia.

At the time of John Carpini's journey, rumours had spread throughout Europe of the existence in Asia of a Christian ruler called Prester John. One of the aims of Carpini's mission was to make contact with this legendary person and gain his help in the fight against the Muslims. The search for Prester John inspired expeditions to the East right into the sixteenth century.

▲ John Carpini and his party had to cross great areas of central Asia, before reaching their destination – the Mongol captial of Karakorum.

▶ The dramatic landscape and the harsh weather conditions made the journey very difficult for Carpini and his men. In all, their journey took over fifteen months.

William Rubruquis
(c. 1215–c. 1295)

William Rubruquis or William of Rubrouck as he is also known, from Flanders, was a monk of the Franciscan Order. In 1253 he was sent by King Louis IX of France on a mission to see the Great Khan Möngke of Tartary in Mongolia. Louis IX had heard that there were Christians living there and wanted to make contact with them. William travelled with gifts from Louis IX for the Great Khan.

▲ The cold, windswept plains and sand dunes of Mongolia were quite unlike anything Rubruquis had seen at home in his native Flanders.

The journey overland across Europe and Asia was long and tiring. Supplies ran short, and he and his companions were forced to eat some of the food they were carrying as presents for the Great Khan. They suffered greatly from frostbite because they wore sandals. When they reached Tartary they were welcomed at the Great Khan's court near Karakorum. At the court they found Christian priests and several Europeans, including a French jeweller.

After seven months at court, William left for home, where he presented the King with a written report of his travels.

One of the discoveries that William Rubruquis made on his travels was that the Caspian Sea was not joined to the Arctic Ocean, as had been believed up until that time.

▶ Franciscan monks were used to travelling and teaching people about Christianity, but few journeyed as far as William Rubruquis.

Marco Polo
(c. 1254–1324)

Marco Polo came from a family of travellers. His father, Niccolò, and uncle, Matteo, were both Venetian merchants who had travelled to Cathay (China) on trading expeditions in the 1260s. In 1271 they made a return visit, taking young Marco with them.

They arrived at the court of Kublai Khan, the Mongol ruler of Cathay. They stayed for twenty-four years and made huge fortunes as traders. Marco won the trust of Kublai Khan, who sent him on a series of journeys to India, Burma (now officially known as Myanma), Ceylon (Sri Lanka) and southeast Asia.

Marco Polo returned to Venice in 1295, but he was captured by the Genoese during a battle between Venice and Genoa. While in prison, he wrote a detailed account of his travels in the East. The Venetians were amazed by Marco Polo's tales of Kublai Khan's palace, which was so huge that it could seat 6,000 people for a meal. Marco Polo's travels caused new interest in exploration and trade among the people of Venice, which went on to become the centre of world trade.

One of the big surprises for Europeans in Marco Polo's book was his description of how advanced Chinese civilization was. When Europe was still trading in gold and silver, China already had paper money. China also had a well-organized postal system, whereas in Europe it was impossible to send a letter and be sure that it would arrive.

▼ This picture from a medieval book shows Marco Polo arriving at Hormuz, at the entrance to the Persian Gulf. He has brought elephants from India.

Ibn Battuta
(1304-1368)

Ibn Battuta was the greatest of all Muslim explorers; he spent thirty years travelling in Asia and Africa. Born in 1304, at Tangier in Morocco, he discovered his taste for travel at the age of 21 when he went on a pilgrimage to the holy city of Mecca. This required a difficult journey by camel across North Africa, by boat across the Red Sea, and finally on foot through the Arabian desert. From Mecca he continued eastwards to Persia (present-day Iran), returning to Mecca to study Islamic law.

He wanted to go to India next, but the only boat he could find was sailing south, down the east coast of Africa. He visited present-day Somalia, Kenya and Tanzania and later visited Egypt, Syria and Palestine (including Jerusalem). Ibn Battuta then travelled northwards to the Crimea and southern Russia, and continued east through Afghanistan. At last, in 1333, he reached India, where the Sultan of Delhi made him ambassador to China. In the following years he continued to travel all over Asia.

▲ Ibn Battuta travelled across the Sahara to the lush hills and valleys of West Africa on his fourth journey.

In all, it has been estimated that Ibn Battuta must have travelled over 120,000 kilometres. No wonder he is described in the introduction to the book about his life as 'the great traveller of our age'!

→ 1st Expedition
--→ 2nd Expedition
→ 3rd Expedition
→ 4th Expedition

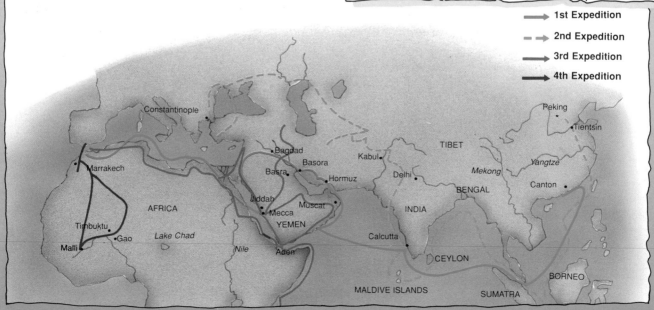

Vasco da Gama

(c. 1460–1524)

Vasco da Gama, a Portuguese sea-captain, was the first European to travel by sea to India. In 1497 he was was chosen by King Manuel I of Portugal to lead an expedition to find a sea route to India. Portugal was keen to control the valuable trade with the East.

Da Gama's party included four ships and 170 men, many of whom were convicted criminals. The part of the route as far as the Cape of Good Hope was already known, but it was a troubled voyage. Da Gama had to cope with a mutiny, fierce storms and the effects of scurvy among the crew. The ships sailed up the east coast of Africa before striking east across the Indian Ocean. Da Gama was guided by local pilots who advised him on the weather conditions. The ships finally arrived at Calicut (now Kozhikode) on India's southwestern coast in May 1498. Da Gama made a trade agreement with the ruler before sailing for home.

The return journey too was hard. More men died of scurvy, leaving only fifty-five to return home.

Da Gama returned to India in 1502 on a mission to secure further trading rights. He died of a fever in 1521 after his third voyage to India.

Scurvy was a disease that killed thousands of sailors on long voyages until a way of preventing it was discovered in the eighteenth century. Doctors discovered that scurvy could be prevented by making sure that fresh fruit and vegetables or fruit juice (which all contain vitamin C) were provided on long voyages.

▶ Vasco da Gama paid homage to the local ruler at Calicut, India, in 1498.

Ludovico de Varthema
(c. 1461-1517)

Born in the Italian city of Bologna, Ludovico de Varthema achieved two exploring 'firsts'. He was the first European to write about the Islamic ceremonies at Mecca, and the first to reach the Spice Islands of the East Indies.

He set out on his travels in 1502. He went first through Egypt to Arabia where he studied Arabic. He then joined a pilgrim caravan to Mecca. He planned to go on to India, but was arrested by Muslim soldiers and imprisoned as a Christian spy.

After his release, he resumed his journey. He travelled across the Indian Ocean to India and then returned to the great trading centre of Hormuz, in present-day Iran. Here, Ludovico de Varthema teamed up with a merchant, Junair, and together they travelled through India, Ceylon (present-day Sri Lanka) and Burma (now Myanma). In 1506 they set sail for the Spice Islands of Malacca, Sumatra and the Moluccas.

The rest of his active life was spent as a soldier in the service of Portugal and he visited many of the Portuguese outposts on the east coast of Africa. He retired to Rome where he lived until his death in 1517.

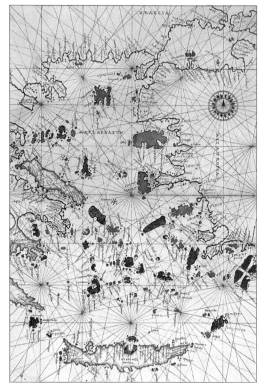

▲ This map of Asia Minor and its many islands was drawn in the sixteenth century.

The Spice Islands, now part of Indonesia, are a string of islands between Borneo and New Guinea in the southern Pacific. Their nutmeg, mace and other spices were highly prized in Europe. The wish to gain control of the rich trade in these spices was one of the reasons why many Europeans made dangerous expeditions to find new routes to the East.

▶ Pepper is gathered by the local people in the Spice Islands. The trade in spices brought travellers here from all over the world.

Isbrand Ides
(born c. 1660)

In 1682, a new Tsar of Russia came to the throne who became known as 'Peter the Great'. At that time, Russia was a poor country with little contact with the rest of the world. Peter saw that if his empire was to prosper, it must begin to trade with countries to both the east and west. One of Russia's most valuable natural resources was fur, especially sable, from Siberia. But Russian trappers and traders roamed central Asia, where the borders between Russia and China were uncertain, and came into conflict with the Chinese. Small clashes threatened to turn into a war, and so, in 1689, Peter the Great decided to send an expedition to sign a treaty with the Chinese. He chose an experienced Danish traveller, Isbrand Ides, to lead the expedition. Ides took a Dutch painter, Cornelius de Bruyn, with him.

They travelled across central Asia to Nerchinsk, close to where the borders of Russia, Mongolia and China meet. There, they met a Chinese party, with a French Roman Catholic priest to act as interpreter. The result was a treaty that set out the areas over which Russian and Chinese trappers could work. With his duty done, Ides continued to explore the eastern part of the Russian empire before returning to Russia in 1694. He wrote a book about his journey which was published in 1704.

▼ The border between Russia and China was not clear, and in vast areas of wilderness such as this, trappers from both countries would meet and fight.

The French Roman Catholic priest who helped to secure the treaty between Russia and China was one of a number of priests from France, known as the Jesuits, who travelled to China in the 17th century in the hope of bringing Christianity to the East. They helped to greatly increase European knowledge of that still-mysterious country.

Carsten Niebuhr
(1733–1815)

Carsten Niebuhr, a German explorer, had the terrible experience of watching all of his companions die on an expedition, leaving him to find his way home alone.

It happened during a six-year journey through the Middle East between 1761 and 1767. Niebuhr had set out with a Danish expedition to explore Egypt, Arabia and Syria. Niebuhr prepared himself thoroughly by studying mathematics – for navigation – and Arabic. The party included an Arabic scholar, a botanist, an artist and a surgeon.

At first, the expedition went well. The party landed in Egypt and explored the Nile before going on to the Red Sea port of Jiddah. They had hoped to travel overland to Mecca, but they were refused permission and they went instead to Yemen. They made a number of journeys inland, making maps of the area and sketching wildlife. But the Arabic scholar and the botanist both died of fever.

The survivors travelled on to India, but the artist and the surgeon died on the voyage. Niebuhr was now on his own. It took him three years to make his way back to Europe.

▲ The Nile, which Niebuhr explored in the 1760s, winds its way through Egypt and Sudan.

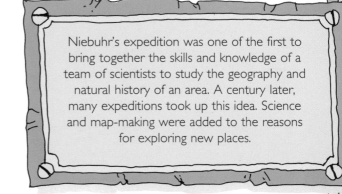

Niebuhr's expedition was one of the first to bring together the skills and knowledge of a team of scientists to study the geography and natural history of an area. A century later, many expeditions took up this idea. Science and map-making were added to the reasons for exploring new places.

▼ Mountains and desert plains met Niebuhr and his companions in Yemen. Niebuhr was the first European to map this area.

Nikolai Przhevalsky
(1839-1888)

Nikolai Przhevalsky was a Russian army officer who made four major expeditions to explore central Asia between 1871 and his death in 1888.

He set out on his first journey in November 1870, from near Lake Baikal in Siberia, close to the Russian border with Mongolia.

Przhevalsky's party travelled across the Gobi Desert almost as far as present-day Beijing in China. He travelled up the Huang He River and explored northern China. He even went a little way into Tibet, which was then completely unknown to the outside world.

In 1879-80, on Przhevalsky's fourth journey, he entered Tibet. But when he was about 275 kilometres from the capital, Lhasa, Tibetan guards made him turn back. He was very disappointed that he could not explore further.

This journey was to be his last. He was returning home after travelling in the mountains between Mongolia and Tibet when he fell ill and died. The town of Karakol in southern Russia, where he died, was renamed Przhevalsk after him.

Although not scientifically trained, Przhevalsky was a keen naturalist, and made a collection of plants and animals during his travels. Among the animals Przhevalsky brought back from his third expedition were wild camels and a rare breed of wild horse, which is now named after him.

◀ The horse that was named after Przhevalsky is the only species of wild horse that still survives.

Francis Younghusband
(1863-1942)

Francis Younghusband, a British army officer, explored central Asia and Tibet.

He set out from Beijing in China in 1887, and travelled westwards across the Gobi Desert by an unknown route. After covering 2,000 kilometres in six weeks, he arrived at the oasis and trading centre of Hami, on the western edge of the Gobi. Here, he picked up an old trading route which took him to Shufu, in the foothills of the Karakoram Mountains, north of the Himalayas.

The way ahead, across the mountains, was unexplored but Younghusband found local guides to help him. They had to make crossing-places in the rivers by throwing rocks into them. As they reached the Mustagh Pass, they found their route blocked by a huge glacier. Younghusband sent the guides back with the ponies, while he and three others climbed up the glacier and down the other side by cutting steps in the ice with their picks. Three days later, they arrived in Kashmir.

▲ No European had explored the mountains of Tibet before Younghusband. Like many later explorers he had to rely on the expert knowledge of guides from the local villages to help him find his way through the dangerous terrain.

Younghusband worked for the British government in India from 1890 to 1909 and became an expert on Tibet. He led a British expedition to Lhasa, the capital of Tibet, in 1902 and later organized a survey of the country. This work earned him a knighthood in 1904.

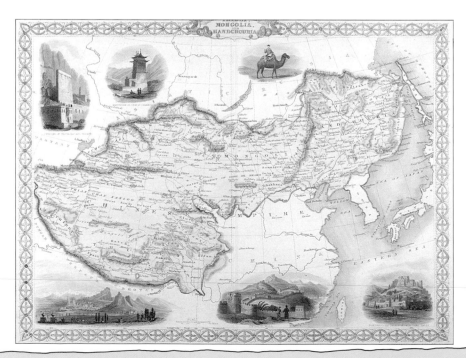

▶ This map of 1845 is similar to the ones Younghusband would have seen before his expedition. It lacks very much detail as little was known about the area.

Sven Hedin
(1865-1952)

Sven Hedin was a Swedish explorer who spent thirty years of his life on expeditions in central Asia and China.

One of his most important discoveries was made on an expedition to the Taklamakan Desert in western China between 1894 and 1897. He solved the mystery surrounding the position of Lop-Nur, a salt-lake basin, which seemed to have moved since it was first mapped by the ancient Chinese. Hedin found that the Tarim, the river supplying the lake, changed its course frequently, causing the lake to move its position too.

In 1898 Hedin discovered the lost city of Lou Lan in the sand. In 1905 he returned to Tibet, produced the first detailed map of the country and found the source of the River Indus.

Hedin continued travelling until he was well into his sixties and wrote many books about his great journeys which made him one of the best-known twentieth-century explorers.

During his expeditions, Sven Hedin made a collection of over 8,000 rock samples and relics of ancient civilizations. These are now in the Sven Hedin Foundation in Stockholm, Sweden.

▼ Hedin rides a Bactrian camel, the native beast of burden of central Asia.

Willem Jansz
(born c. 1570)

Willem Jansz, a Dutch navigator, was the first European to land in Australia and make contact with native Australians. In 1605 he set out from Amsterdam for New Guinea, in the Pacific, in his ship, the *Duifken*, which means 'little dove'.

After following the southern coast of New Guinea, Jansz either lost his way or was blown off course. Whatever the reason, he headed south and in March 1606 he reached the northernmost tip of Australia, which is now called Cape York.

Following the coast southwards into the Gulf of Carpentaria – the big 'bite' out of Australia's northern coast – Jansz reached a headland which is now called Duifken Point, after his ship. The land was desert and did not look very interesting, but Jansz decided to send a landing party ashore. They were set upon by Aboriginals (native Australians), described by Jansz as wild, cruel, savages, and several of the Dutch party were killed. The rest retreated, and Jansz sailed back north.

▲ This map of Australia was made in the 1660s, when the land was known as New Holland. The unexplored eastern coast is not shown.

Willem Jansz never knew that he had been the first European to set foot on the Australian mainland. To the end of his life, he believed that he had landed on another part of New Guinea. Later Dutch explorers were to give Australia its first European name, New Holland.

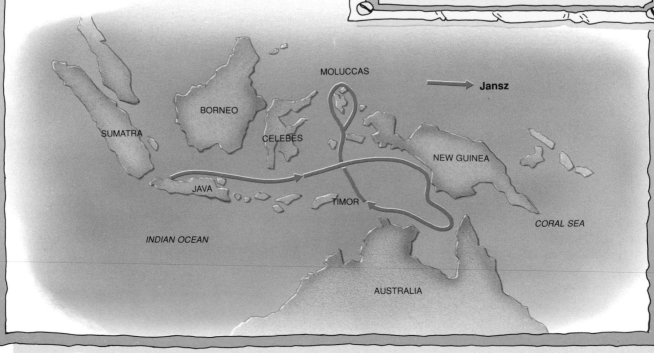

Abel Janszoon Tasman
(c. 1603-1659)

In the seventeenth century the Dutch became the most powerful trading nation in the East. They organized many voyages of exploration in the South Seas.

In August 1642 Abel Tasman, a Dutch navigator, was put in charge of an expedition to the 'South Land', as the Dutch called Australia. He set sail from Batavia (now Jakarta) on the island of Java.

Three months after he started, Tasman sighted a land of dense forests. He named it Van Diemen's Land, we know it today as the island of Tasmania.

Sailing eastwards, Tasman next discovered New Zealand, naming it Staten Land. On his way back to the East Indies he discovered Tonga and Fiji. Tasman did not realize it, but he had sailed half way around Australia.

On his return from a second voyage, Tasman reported that Australia looked wild and barren, and the people poor and hostile. Such a land was unlikely to offer the rich trading opportunities that the Dutch were looking for. This probably put them off the idea of founding settlements there. It was left to Britain to set up colonies in Australia 150 years later.

▼ In Fiji, Tasman found a land of lush vegetation and people who travelled in outrigger canoes.

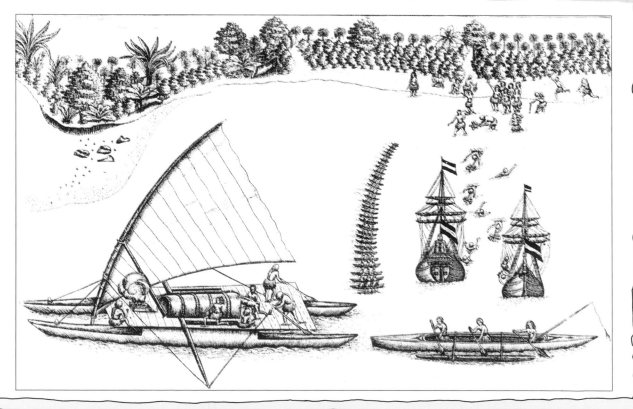

Matthew Flinders
(1774-1814)

Since Captain James Cook's voyage of 1768-71, the British government had viewed Australia as a possible new colony. But there was little detailed information about the continent. So in 1801, Captain Matthew Flinders, of the Royal Navy, was sent on an expedition to Australia to survey the coast.

Flinders already knew Australia. In an exploratory voyage (1795-9) with another sailor, George Bass, he had sailed round Tasmania (then known as Van Diemen's Land), proving that it was an island. A smaller island off the coast is named after him.

In 1801, he set out eastwards from Cape Leeuwin at the southwestern tip of Australia. Flinders successfully charted the Australian coast. On his voyage home to England, his ship was wrecked on a coral reef, fortunately near a sandbank where the crew camped out. With two others, Flinders set out in a open boat to fetch help. After two months he and his crew set sail again. Disaster struck once more when his ship called at the French island of Mauritius in the Indian Ocean. Because Britain and France were at war, Flinders, accused of spying, was imprisoned for six years. He reached home, at last, in 1810.

▼ When Flinders's ship, the *Porpoise*, was wrecked, he and his men had to take to open boats.

After returning to England, Flinders spent four years writing a book about his voyage round Australia. It was published on 19 July, 1814. He died the same day.

Charles Sturt
(1795–1869)

Charles Sturt was a British army officer who was sent to Australia in 1827. He became one of the first explorers of eastern Australia.

Sturt led three expeditions into the interior of Australia. In 1828, he travelled 480 kilometres westwards from Sydney and discovered a river which he named Darling after the governor of New South Wales. The river water was too salty to drink so Sturt had to return.

In 1829 he set out again, following the Murrumbidgee River west by boat. He discovered the junction of the Murrumbidgee with another river, which he named the Murray. He followed this to its mouth near Adelaide.

Sturt's third trip (1844-5) was his most adventurous. He led a party of sixty from Adelaide up the Murray and Darling rivers. He then headed northwards into the desert. After an exhausting journey in the heat and drought, they found a small water source. It was high summer, so Sturt decided to stay there until he could lead his party back in the cooler winter months. It was March 1846 before they reached Adelaide again, after a terrible journey. They were all exhausted, and Sturt had gone blind. However, their journey had taken them within 240 kilometres of the centre of Australia.

The first British settlements on mainland Australia were along the southeastern coast – the area now known as New South Wales. The rest of the vast continent was unknown territory, but there were rumours that it contained, somewhere in the centre, a great inland sea. The purpose of many early explorations, including Sturt's third journey, was to find this sea.

▼ On the Murray River, Sturt fought with local people who threatened to hold up their progress.

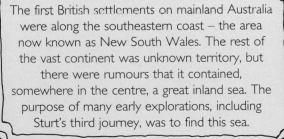

Friedrich Wilhelm Ludwig Leichhardt (1813-1848)

Friedrich Leichhardt was the hero of several epic expeditions across the interior of Australia. He was born in Germany and, after a scientific education, arrived in Australia in 1842.

He set out on his first expedition alone and without equipment. It was a 960-kilometre walk from Sydney to Brisbane. Here, he won support from local businessmen for a more ambitious journey from Brisbane, on the east coast of Australia, to the northern coast. The party set out in August 1844, and when nothing more was heard of them they were feared lost. But Leichhardt and his men turned up at Port Essington, near Darwin, in December 1845, starving and in rags but still alive. They had travelled over 4,800 kilometres. For this exploit Leichhardt was awarded the gold medals of the Geographical Societies of both Paris and London.

Leichhardt's next major project was to cross Australia from east to west, starting from the Fitzroy River in Queensland, in eastern Australia, and aiming for Perth, on the west coast. His party set out in February 1848. Apart from a brief message two months later, they were never seen again.

▼ Leichhardt amazed the world when he turned up near Darwin in 1845. Unfortunately, his second journey did not have the same happy ending.

Leichhardt's disappearance remains one of the great mysteries of Australian exploration. Over the years, many expeditions have been mounted tracing his last journey, in the hope of finding the answer. The most recent was in 1953. But the solution remains locked somewhere in the Australian desert.

John McDouall Stuart
(1815-1866)

John McDouall Stuart was a Scot who emigrated to Australia at the age of 20. His first experience of exploration came in 1844 when he took part in Charles Sturt's expedition to central Australia, an area Stuart returned to several times.

In 1860, the government of South Australia offered £10,000 (in those days equal to US$2,500) for the first crossing of Australia from south to north. Stuart attempted the journey three times. He set out on his first expedition in March 1860, but after reaching central Australia he was met by hostile Aboriginals (native Australians) and was forced to turn back. By the time Stuart set off again in November, Burke and Wills (see page 65) had already set out on their successful but doomed expedition. This time, Stuart lost his way and, with his water supplies dwindling, again had to return home.

Stuart's third attempt was successful. He set out from Adelaide in October 1861, and in the following July reached the north coast of Australia, at a point close to where the city of Darwin now stands. By this time, news of the Burke and Wills expedition was known, but the South Australian government gave Stuart a £2,000 ($500) consolation prize.

John McDouall Stuart's south-north route across Australia was used when the first telegraph link between Australia and Europe was established. The cables ran from Adelaide to Darwin and then under the sea to the East Indies.

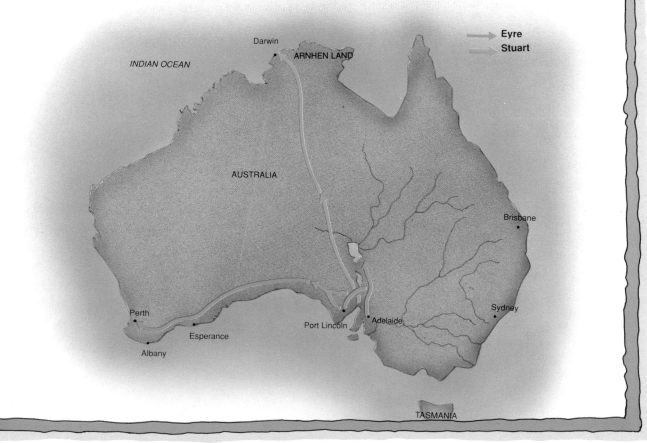

Edward John Eyre
(1815-1901)

Edward John Eyre was an Englishman who emigrated to Australia when he was 18 years old. He made many journeys into the interior of Australia, north and west of Adelaide, trying to find an overland route from Adelaide to Perth. On one such expedition he discovered the huge salt lake, which is named after him.

In February 1841 Eyre, with a friend and three Aboriginals (native Australians), set out westwards from Adelaide. They travelled with pack-horses and sheep. For days their only source of water was dew and the sap of the few plants they could find. Two of the Aboriginals murdered Eyre's friend and stole his supplies, leaving Eyre and the other Aboriginal to carry on across the Nullarbor Plain. Helped by the crew of a French whaling ship, they reached King George's Sound, on the southwest coast of Australia, in July 1841. They had walked over 2,500 kilometres.

▲ Eyre was fortunate to choose a coastal route across the Nullarbor Plain. The crew of a French whaling ship gave him food and water.

The Nullarbor ('treeless') Plain stretches for about 1,530 kilometres along the southern coast of Australia. For almost all the year it is a sunbaked wilderness. But after rain it is covered with masses of short-lived but spectacular flowers. The Perth to Adelaide railway crosses the plain. One 530-kilometre stretch of line is the longest straight railway track in the world.

Robert O'Hara Burke (1820-1861) and William John Wills (1834-1861)

Robert O'Hara Burke was born in County Galway, Ireland and spent his early years as a soldier and policeman. He emigrated to Australia in 1853. With William Wills, he led the first team to cross Australia from south to north.

The party of eighteen men set out from Melbourne on 20 August 1860. They used camels, which were well suited to desert conditions, to carry their supplies. The party set up a base camp at Menindee on the Darling River. Here, Burke's original second-in-command, Landells, quarrelled with Burke and resigned, to be replaced by Wills. So, Burke, Wills and seven men rode on 640 kilometres to Cooper's Creek on the edge of the desert. Then Burke, Wills and two others, Charles Gray and John King, rode north. It was a punishing journey, and food ran short. Finally, in February 1861, after about four months, they reached the mouth of the Flinders River in the Gulf of Carpentaria. Their mission had been successful – but they still had to face the return journey. Heavy rain, shortage of food and sickness held them up, but there was no choice other than to struggle on. Burke and Wills died in June 1861, starved and exhausted.

▲ After Burke died, his companion knew he would soon die too. Only King survived, with the help of some Aboriginals.

When rescue parties finally traced the route taken by Burke and Wills from Cooper's Creek, they found their bodies on what the two explorers had hoped would be a short-cut to safety. Beside Wills was his journal of their last days.

◀ Burke and Wills rest towards the end of their expedition in 1861. Even the camels, used to dry conditions, found it tough going.

Pytheas of Massilia

(c. 300 BC)

The ancient civilizations of the Mediterranean were fascinated with what lay beyond the world they knew. About 330 BC Pytheas of Massilia (present-day Marseilles), a Greek sailor, set out to explore the northwest coast of Europe. He was the first Greek to do so. He hoped to set up new trade routes that would bring tin and amber back to Greece.

Pytheas set out from Cadiz in southern Spain and travelled north along the coast of what is now Portugal. He then continued northwards across the Bay of Biscay and then up the English Channel. He visited the tin mines of Cornwall and other places in Britain. Pytheas was interested in the weather and the tides, and kept notes of what he saw. He was the first to suggest that the moon may have an effect on the tides. He found the weather in northern Europe wet and gloomy. Sailing further north, Pytheas reached northern Norway, or possibly Iceland, which he named 'Thule'. This he described as a land of mystery, hidden in thick mist. Pytheas's own story of his voyage is lost, but historians know about it from other Greek writers.

Pytheas and his sailors were surprised to find how short summer nights are in northern Europe. He met people who told him that this was because it was close to the sleeping place of the sun.

Polybius
(c. 205-c. 120 BC)

Polybius was a Greek soldier whose interest in history led him into exploration. At the age of about 60, he began to research and write a history of the Roman Empire.

Polybius planned to show how the history of one nation influences those around it. He did not rely merely on his opinion or on the writings of others. He began a series of journeys to Asia Minor, Egypt, Italy, France and Spain, tracing the reasons for the spread of the Roman Empire. His careful collection of material provided a model for later historians of how historical research should be carried out. Polybius did not explore unknown territory, but he searched thoroughly for the truth about how the Roman Empire came to be built.

Polybius wrote his history in forty volumes. Only five of these, plus his plan for the whole work, have survived in their original form, but parts of other volumes have been discovered over the years and reprinted.

▲ Polybius was a historian who saw many of the places and events he described. For example, he witnessed the destruction of the North African city of Carthage in 146 BC.

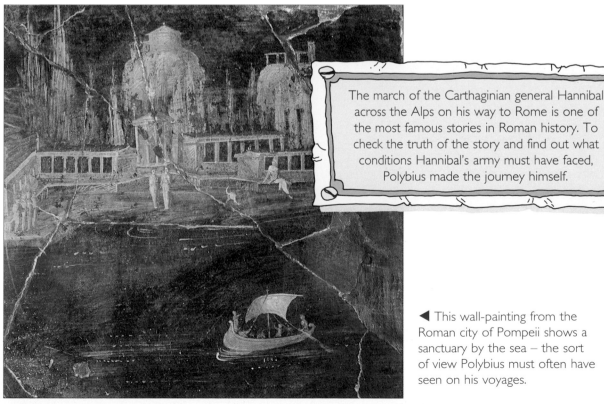

The march of the Carthaginian general Hannibal across the Alps on his way to Rome is one of the most famous stories in Roman history. To check the truth of the story and find out what conditions Hannibal's army must have faced, Polybius made the journey himself.

◄ This wall-painting from the Roman city of Pompeii shows a sanctuary by the sea – the sort of view Polybius must often have seen on his voyages.

Ibn Jubayr
(1145-1217)

In the period from AD 650 to 750, Arab armies fought their way west along the north African coast and northwards into Spain. These Muslim invaders, called Moors, occupied southern Spain until the fifteenth century.

Ibn Jubayr was an Arab born in Spain in 1145. He became secretary to the governor of Granada, but in 1183, at the age of 38, he left the governor's service and set out on his travels, during which he planned to make a pilrimage to the holy city of Mecca.

His travels took two years. He visited Alexandria, Jerusalem, Mecca, Medina, Damascus, Baghdad and Sicily. Two years after his return he set out on a second journey to the eastern Mediterranean. His descriptions of the places he visited give a vivid picture of life in the twelfth-century Arab world.

▼ This map of eastern Mediterranean and northern Africa was drawn some time after Ibn Jubayr made his journeys, but shows the detailed knowledge the Arabic world had of this area.

Muslims are followers of Islam. They are taught that they should try to make a pilgrimage to Mecca at least once in their lives. Many do, but many others are too poor. However, all faithful Muslims pray five times a day, and when they do they turn to face Mecca.

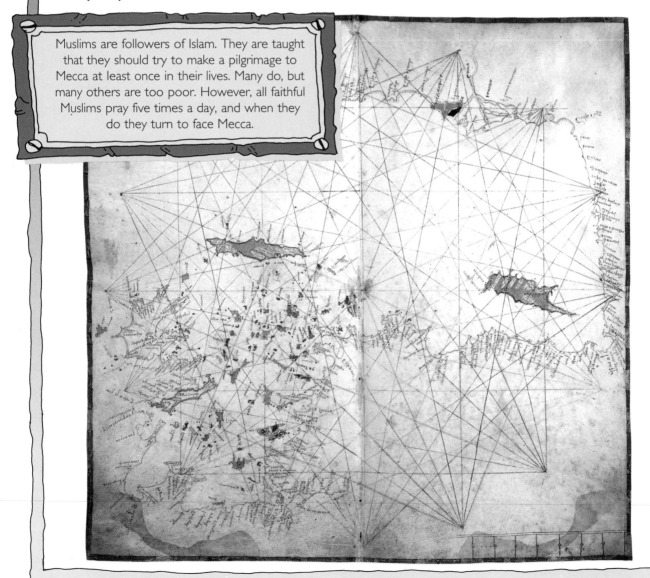

Leif Eriksson
(born AD 970)

Exploration and adventure were in Leif Eriksson's blood. He was the son of the Viking sailor Eric the Red (see page 30), who in around AD 982 discovered Greenland and later settled there. Leif lived in Greenland as a boy, but then moved to Norway. He returned to his homeland in adult life to convert the Greenlanders to Christianity.

According to legend, Leif Eriksson and his crew of thirty-five were blown off course on a voyage to Greenland from Iceland around the year 1000. They drifted westwards until they reached lands they called Helluland and Markland on Canada's eastern coast. Sailing further south, they came to a place which they called 'Vinland' where wild grapes and wheat grew. It is not certain where Vinland was. But in the 1960s remains of a Viking settlement were found on Newfoundland, which shows that these explorers definitely did reach North America.

Eriksson and his crew sailed for home in the spring, and took with them wild grapes and timber as proof of their story. Leif Eriksson later took over from his father as ruler of the Viking settlement in Greenland.

As far as anyone knows, the Vikings made no attempt to settle in 'Vinland', although its mild climate and plentiful food supplies must have been attractive to people used to the harsher conditions of northern Europe and Greenland. Probably the distance from home and the hazards of the long sea journey put the Vikings off.

◄ Eriksson and his party found the lands of North America strange and exotic, with plants and animals adapted to a climate warmer than the freezing temperatures of Greenland.

John Cabot
(c. 1450-c. 1499)

In the fifteenth century, many European navigators believed that 'the Indies' – by which they meant Asia – could be reached by sailing westwards across the Atlantic. One man who tried to do this was John Cabot. He was born in the Italian city of Genoa, but he undertook his first voyage of exploration on orders from King Henry VII of England. He became the first European since the Vikings to reach the mainland of North America.

Cabot sighted land, probably the coast of Nova Scotia, and sailed down the east coast of North America, making frequent landings. In a second expedition two years later, he reached further south, possibly as far as Maryland.

NEWFOUNDLAND

GULF OF
ST LAWRENCE

Halifax

➡ **Cabot**

ATLANTIC OCEAN

▼ It is not known for certain where Cabot landed, but he faced an icy landscape like this one at Ellesmere Island, Canada.

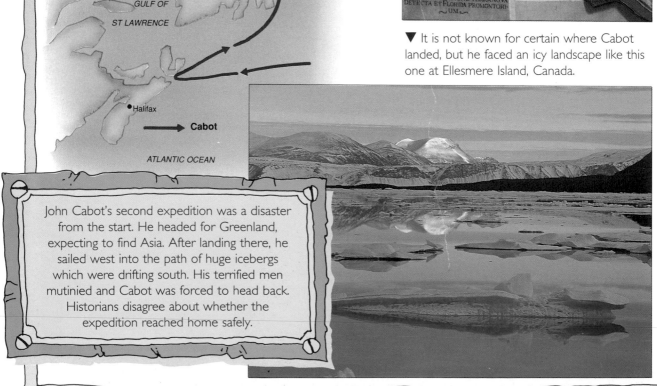

John Cabot's second expedition was a disaster from the start. He headed for Greenland, expecting to find Asia. After landing there, he sailed west into the path of huge icebergs which were drifting south. His terrified men mutinied and Cabot was forced to head back. Historians disagree about whether the expedition reached home safely.

Vasco Núñez de Balboa
(c. 1475-1519)

The Spanish and Portuguese explorations of the West Indies, Central and South America were followed by conquest and settlement. Vasco Núñez de Balboa was among the early Spanish settlers. He first crossed the Atlantic in 1511.

By 1513, Balboa had become governor of Darien, on the Atlantic coast of present-day Panama. He heard stories from the local people that another great ocean lay to the west. So, on 1 September 1513 he led a large expedition to search for it. In the party were 190 Spaniards and 1,000 American Indians to guide them and act as porters and servants. Three weeks later, Balboa looked down on what we now call the Pacific Ocean from the mountains of the Sierra del Darien. His reward was to be proclaimed Governor of the Great South Sea, but his triumph was short-lived. In 1519, jealous of his success, a rival had him arrested, tried for treason and beheaded.

Balboa made his voyage to Darien in 1510 to escape from his debts. A farm he had owned on the island of Hispaniola had proved a failure. He hid himself among the food supplies being loaded aboard two expedition ships. Once the ships were at sea, he took over command.

▼ Balboa rushed into the Pacific Ocean in full armour and claimed it for the King of Spain.

Hernán (Ferdinand) Cortés

(1485-1547)

Hernán Cortés was the most famous of the Spanish conquistadores. Born in Spain, he settled on the West Indian island of Hispaniola in 1504 when he was 19 years old. Seven years later he took part in the conquest of Cuba. Inspired by tales of cities of great wealth, full of gold and jewels, in 1519 Cortés led an expedition to invade Mexico.

Mexico was the land of the Aztecs, who had their capital at Tenochtitlán, where Mexico City now stands. Cortés arrived there in November 1519 and was at first welcomed by the Aztec emperor Montezuma II. The new arrivals filled the people of Tenochtitlán with wonder and were treated as gods.

Cortés, through his cunning, took control of the city and made Montezuma his prisoner. However, the Aztecs revolted against Spanish rule and a long struggle between the Aztecs and the Spaniards began. Cortés and his men finally captured the city in August 1521.

Cortés continued to explore Mexico and established Spanish rule there. In 1535 he travelled further afield, into what is now California, but bad weather forced his party to turn back.

Tenochtitlán, the Aztec capital, was a city built on man-made islands on a marsh in the middle of a lake. The Aztecs moved around it by boat along a network of canals. In the centre was the pyramid-shaped Great Temple, where prisoners were killed and then hurled down the steps as human sacrifices to the gods.

◀ This seventeenth-century painting shows Cortés visiting Montezuma II in the Aztec capital. The Aztecs had never seen horses and guns before, and thought that the Spanish must be gods of some kind.

Giovanni da Verrazano
(c. 1485-c. 1528)

Giovanni da Verrazano was a sailor from Florence in Italy, but he made his career sailing in French ships. In 1523 he set out from Dieppe, France, in his ship *La Dauphine* (the Dolphin) on an expedition to seek a way from the Atlantic to the Pacific, which he believed existed across North America.

Verrazano first sighted North America at Cape Fear, in what is now North Carolina, in March. He then worked his way slowly northwards, to investigate Pamlico Sound and Albemarle Sound to see if they led to the Pacific. Finding that these were merely inlets from the sea, he went further north and discovered the much larger expanse of water now called Chesapeake Bay. When they explored the peninsula that extends south into the Atlantic, his party looked westwards and saw what they thought was the Indian Ocean. They were wrong, of course, as they discovered when they explored further. Undaunted, they went on surveying the coast as far north as Newfoundland before turning for home. Verrazano arrived back in France in July 1524.

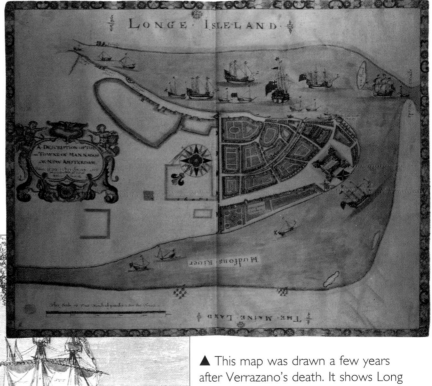

▲ This map was drawn a few years after Verrazano's death. It shows Long Island and New York.

The early makers of maps of North America called Chesapeake Bay 'the Sea of Verrazano'. Verrazano's name is still commemorated by the Verrazano-Narrows Bridge, built in 1964, which crosses the entrance to New York harbour – one of the inlets he explored.

▶ Verrazano's ship, *La Dauphine*, in Newport Harbour.

Jacques Cartier
(1491-1557)

For over five centuries, explorers tried to find a short route from Europe to Asia along the northern coast of North America. This route became known as the Northwest Passage. One of the first to investigate this possibility was a French explorer, Jacques Cartier.

Cartier set out in April 1534 from his home port of St Malo in Brittany with two small ships and ninety-nine men. He reached the Gulf of St Lawrence, on Canada's east coast, in May. From there, he tried in vain to find a channel that would lead him across North America, and was forced to return home.

The next year he set out again. He sailed up the St Lawrence River as far as the present site of Quebec. Cartier used small boats to explore a further 320 kilometres upstream and arrived at an Indian village called Hochelega. Cartier climbed a nearby mountain to find out what lay upstream, and saw some fearsome rapids that would prevent the boats from going any further. Again, Cartier returned to France.

Cartier had been told by the Indians at Hochelega of a country called Saguenay that was said to be rich in valuable minerals. In 1541 Cartier made a third expedition to find it. On his return to France in 1542, he discovered that the gems he brought with him and had taken to be diamonds were only quartz.

▲ Cartier failed in his ambition to find the Northwest Passage and in his search for valuable minerals. But he had a greater success than these in opening up Canada to the Europeans. In this sense, his influence still lives on today.

Jacques Cartier gave the name Mont Real (Mount Royal) to the mountain he climbed near the village of Hochelega. This in turn gave the name Montreal to the city founded by French settlers a century later in 1642. Montreal is Canada's largest city.

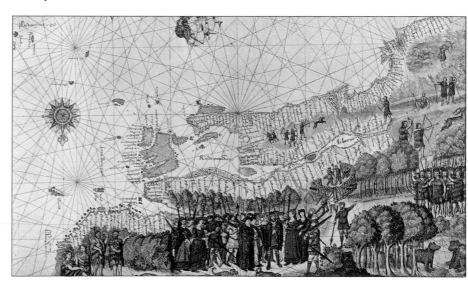

Fernando de Soto
(c. 1496-1542)

Fernando de Soto was born in Spain and had already lived a full life of adventure before he led the expedition for which he is famous.

His first expedition was to Darien in Panama in 1519. In 1528 he explored the coasts of Central America, and accomapnied Pizarro (see page 98) to Peru in 1530.

De Soto had heard tales of the gold to be found in Florida, and in 1538 he set out with 600 men and over one hundred horses in four ships. They landed in Tampa Bay, Florida, in May 1539 and marched northwards in search of gold.

They marched for nearly four years, travelling up the Georgia River, across the Blue Ridge Mountains and along the Alabama River. There were skirmishes with Indians and, in southern Alabama, a full-scale battle. The Indians retreated, but left many of de Soto's men dead.

In May 1541 the party came upon the

▲ Landing at Tampa de Soto faced a long march; many men would die from disease or starvation.

great Mississippi River, and crossed it close to where Memphis, Tennessee, stands today. Further exploration failed to find gold, so the Spaniards turned south and made their way home down the Mississippi. De Soto fell victim to the fevers of the Mississippi swamps, and died on the banks of the river. The rest of the party continued to the coast and eventually returned to Cuba.

The Mississippi, with its tributary the Missouri, is 6,020 kilometres long, North America's longest waterway. It flows into the Gulf of Mexico. Memphis, the state of Tennessee's largest city, stands where de Soto crossed the river.

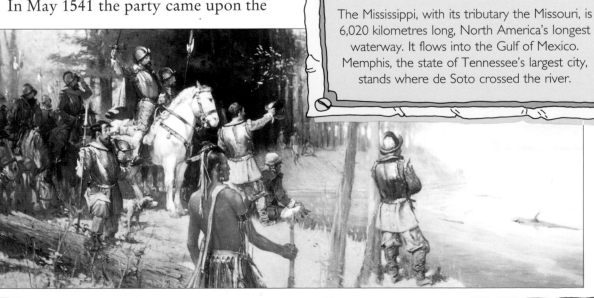

Francisco Vasquez de Coronado
(c. 1510-1564)

The Spanish conquerors of Central and South America had very little idea of what lay to the north. The voyages of Christopher Columbus and others had failed to find the coast of North America. What mysterious land, if any, was there to the north of Mexico?

Francisco Vasquez de Coronado was the first European to find out. Born in Spain in 1510, he settled in Mexico when he was 25. In 1540 he was sent by Cortés to lead an expedition northwards to investigate reports of wealthy cities, known as Cibola in what is now New Mexico. The stories came from American Indians whom the Spanish had befriended or taken prisoner. The Indians probably thought that the conquistadores would move on in search of riches and leave them in peace. The 'cities' that Coronado found turned out to be poor Indian villages.

Coronado sent small parties out to explore the Rio Grande, northeastern Arizona and the Grand Canyon. As winter approached, he set out again, having heard of a rich country further north. He crossed the Great Plains, but found no riches and had to return to Mexico disappointed.

▲ Coronado saw the superb scenery of the Grand Canyon, and heards of bison on the prairies beyond, but found none of the riches he hoped for.

It thought that the North American Indians were introduced to horses through Coronado's expedition. Horses may have escaped from their encampments and returned to the wild, where they were later captured by the Indians.

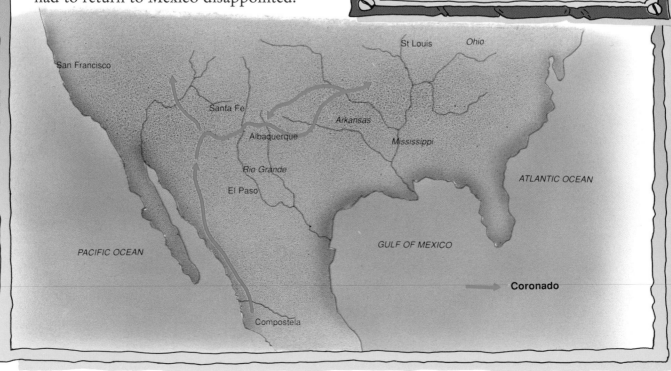

St Louis Ohio

San Francisco

Santa Fe

Arkansas

Albaquerque

Mississippi

Rio Grande

El Paso

ATLANTIC OCEAN

PACIFIC OCEAN

GULF OF MEXICO

➤ **Coronado**

Compostela

John Davis
(c. 1550-1605)

John Davis made three voyages to the Arctic to try to find the Northwest Passage. His first was in 1585. His ships sailed up the west coast of Greenland and across to Baffin Island. This strait is now named after him. He discovered the inlet now called Cumberland Sound on the southwest coast of Baffin Island. He believed that this might be the beginning of the Northwest Passage, but winter began to close in and he had to head for home before investigating further.

Next year he returned to explore the islands and inlets as far south as Newfoundland. Oddly, he did not return to Cumberland Sound. This was left until his third, 1587, expedition, when he discovered that Cumberland Sound was merely an inlet from the sea.

John Davis was a scientist at heart, and kept detailed records of his voyages which were to prove valuable to later Arctic explorers. His charts of the Arctic waters off northern Canada were still in use two centuries later.

Although his Arctic adventures ended in 1587, Davis continued to explore elsewhere. He was killed by Japanese pirates off Sumatra in 1605.

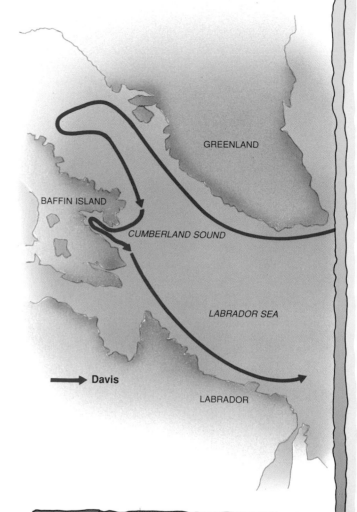

GREENLAND

BAFFIN ISLAND

CUMBERLAND SOUND

LABRADOR SEA

→ Davis

LABRADOR

One of John Davis's later discoveries was of the Falkland Islands off the southeastern coast of South America. He sighted these in 1592 while on a voyage to the Pacific. But he did not land. The first sailor to land on the Falklands was a Dutchman, Sebald de Vert, in 1598.

◀ Icebergs off Greenland shine in the autumn sun. Davis could sail in these conditions, but had to leave for home when winter began.

Samuel de Champlain
(1567–1635)

Samuel de Champlain was a French explorer who did more than anyone else to establish French influence in Canada. He first went there in 1603 and followed Jacques Cartier's route up the St Lawrence River. Unlike many other European explorers, Champlain made efforts to befriend the native American Indians he met. These were the Hurons. On a later expedition in 1608, Champlain founded a new settlement deep in Huron country at Quebec. He took the name from an Indian word meaning 'the place where the river narrows'. Quebec is still the centre of French-speaking Canada.

The Hurons were at war with the stronger neighbouring tribe, the Iroquois, and Champlain offered his Indian friends help against their enemies. In return the Hurons guided Champlain in his exploration of Canada. Over the next few years he explored the Richelieu and Ottawa rivers, reaching the eastern shores of the Great Lakes. He hoped that these would provide a route across North America to the Pacific, but he never put this idea to the test.

Champlain made his home in Quebec, and became governor of 'New France', which was the French name for Canada.

The Iroquois never forgot that the French had sided with their enemies, the Hurons. A century later the Iroquois sided with the British in their war with France for control of Canada.

▶ Champlain joined the Hurons in their fight against the Iroquois. The Iroquois fled when Champlain killed two chiefs with his gun.

Henry Hudson
(died 1611)

In 1607 Henry Hudson was sent by the Muscovy Company, a group involved in trade with Russia, to find a route to China by sailing due north. No one knew that ice covered the polar region. It was thought that the Arctic ice was only a narrow strip. Hudson sailed to the north of Spitsbergen, reaching the 80th parallel. This was further north than anyone had been before. Unable to sail further because of the pack ice, Hudson was forced to turn back.

On his second voyage in 1609, Hudson sailed north again, this time crossing the Barents Sea. However, he was gain forced back by the ice. He then turned west to try to find an alternative route via the Northwest Passage. He sailed down the coast of North America as far as what was to be called the Hudson River. He sailed up the river but failed to find a route to the Pacific.

Starting in 1610, Hudson's final voyage took him again to the Arctic region. His decision to spend the winter at Hudson Bay proved fatal. Food ran short, the crew mutinied, and Hudson was abandoned in an open boat.

▲ At the end of his third expedition, Hudson, his son and five of his crew were cast adrift in an open boat. They were never seen again.

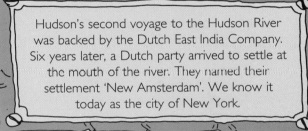

Hudson's second voyage to the Hudson River was backed by the Dutch East India Company. Six years later, a Dutch party arrived to settle at the mouth of the river. They named their settlement 'New Amsterdam'. We know it today as the city of New York.

▼ In 1609, Hudson met Mohawk Indians, who told him that there was no way through the Appalachian Mountains to the Pacific.

William Baffin
(1584-1622)

Nothing is known about William Baffin's life until, at the age of 28, he sailed on his first expedition to find the Northwest Passage. He lived ten more years, and made six more voyages, visiting the Arctic five times.

He set out on his fifth Arctic expedition in March 1616 with plans to explore the Davis Strait as a possible route to the Pacific. Baffin sailed through the strait into Baffin Bay. Sailing south, Baffin found a possible start of the Northwest Passage at Lancaster Sound, but as the days went by he became more and more disheartened. Finally, he became convinced that the Northwest Passage did not exist. He wrote on his return, 'There is no passage nor hope of passage in the north of Davis Strait.'

▲ Baffin Bay lies to the west of Greenland. However, Baffin only explored the bay named after him on his fifth expedition to the Arctic.

▼One day Baffin noted in his journal that the compass had gone wild. He must have been close to the North Pole.

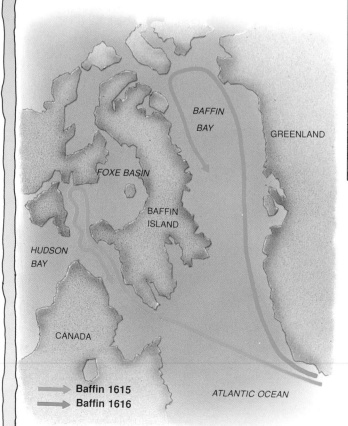

BAFFIN BAY

GREENLAND

FOXE BASIN

BAFFIN ISLAND

HUDSON BAY

CANADA

→ Baffin 1615
→ Baffin 1616

ATLANTIC OCEAN

Baffin acted as the pilot, not the leader, of the expeditions in which he took part. He was thus able to devote his time to navigation and observation. When two later explorers, James Clark Ross and William Parry, followed Baffin's route in the 1820s they marvelled at the accuracy of his charts.

René Robert Cavelier de La Salle
(1643-1687)

Born in the French city of Rouen, France, La Salle arrived in Canada in 1668. At first he earned his living by trading in furs around Lake Ontario. Later he gained the backing of the French king, Louis XIV, to explore further.

La Salle's most important expedition was in 1682. Accompanied by a small party of fellow Frenchmen and Indian guides, he set out from Lake Michigan. He travelled light, on foot or by canoe. He had to drag the canoes across snow-covered country to the Illinois River. He sailed down this until he reached the Mississippi and continued the voyage down river until they came upon the great Mississippi Delta, where the river runs into the Gulf of Mexico. La Salle took possession of the whole valley for France, and named it Louisiana in honour of the French king.

La Salle set out again in 1684 but the voyage was a disaster. He tried for two years to find the Mississippi, without success. His men revolted and one of them shot him; they struggled to the Mississippi on their own.

▲ La Salle claims the lower Mississippi Valley for Louis XIV of France, and names the land Louisiana.

Louisiana remained under French rule until 1769, when it was transferred to Spain. France regained control in 1800, but three years later the state was sold to the United States – a deal known as the Louisiana Purchase. French place names throughout this part of the United States, such as New Orleans and St Louis, are reminders of the days of French ownership.

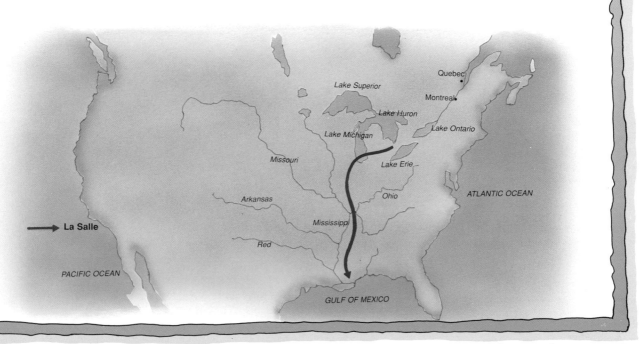

Jean François de Galaup, Comte de la Pérouse (1741-1788)

In 1785 la Pérouse sailed from the port of Brest, with orders from the king of France to explore the northern Pacific coasts of Asia and America, investigate the Northwest Passage, and conduct scientific experiments in the Pacific. By September 1787 he had completed the first two tasks. This is known because, when he reached the Siberian port of Petropavlovsk, he sent one of his men back to France by land with the journals, plans and maps of the expedition up to that point. Letters that La Pérouse sent home from the Pacific in passing ships show that he visited Samoa and other islands, and finally Australia, where he met some English settlers. His ships set sail from Australia in March 1788. After that, there was silence.

The mystery was solved in 1826 when the wreckage of La Pérouse's two ships was found on rocks in the New Hebrides islands (now Vanuatu) east of Australia. There had been no survivors.

▼ La Pérouse and his men fight the people of one of the Pacific islands that they visited.

The history of Europe and the whole world might have been very different if a young Corsican had succeeded in his attempt to join in La Pérouse's expedition. Napoleon Bonaparte, a young officer cadet in the French army, had applied to take part. He was turned down, saving the future Emperor of France, from an early death on a remote Pacific Island.

Alexander Mackenzie
(1764-1820)

Until the 1790s, the interior of northern Canada was a blank on the map. The explorer who started to fill in the white space was Alexander Mackenzie, a fur trader who had emigrated to Canada from Scotland as a boy.

Mackenzie made two journeys to try to find a westward river route across North America. Believing that he would reach the Pacific within a week, in June 1789 he set out by canoe from the Great Slave Lake in the Northwest Territories. He followed the river that flowed westwards from it for over 1,600 kilometres. Travelling northwest, Mackenzie reached the mouth of the river at the Arctic Ocean, not the Pacific.

His second journey to reach the Pacific began in 1792. This time he took a more southerly route from the Great Slave Lake along the Peace River through the Rocky Mountains. To survive the winter, his party built a fort on the banks of the river. When spring came, they pushed on again. Often, they had to carry their canoes through dense forest to avoid canyons and rapids. Using information from Indians they met on their journey, they finally reached the Pacific.

The first European to reach the Pacific by an overland route, Mackenzie was nevertheless disappointed that the route was clearly unsuitable for traffic.

▲ After reaching the Pacific by land, Mackenzie returned to his old life as a fur trader. He eventually retired to Scotland.

The river flowing from the Great Slave Lake to the Arctic Ocean down which Mackenzie sailed in 1792 is now named after him. Mackenzie, who had hoped that it would lead to the Pacific Ocean, had named it the River of Disappointment.

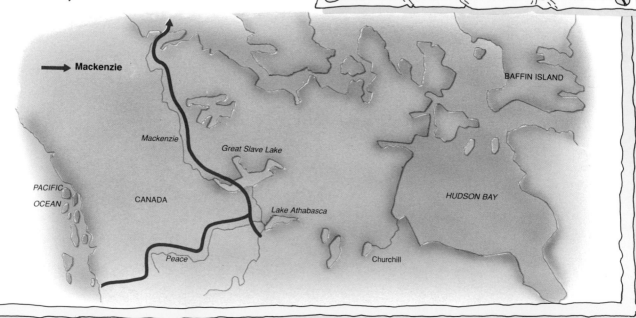

Mackenzie

BAFFIN ISLAND

Mackenzie

Great Slave Lake

PACIFIC OCEAN

CANADA

Lake Athabasca

HUDSON BAY

Peace

Churchill

William Clark (1770-1838)
& Meriwether Lewis (1774-1809)

This famous pair led the first successful overland expedition across the United States. Their party of forty-five set out from St Louis, Missouri, on 14 May 1804. They travelled up the Missouri River by boat. By November they were in what is now North Dakota, close to the Canadian border, where they set up camp for the winter.

During this time they built up many friendships with local Indians. One chief of the Mandan tribe described a large river, which Lewis and Clark thought must be the Columbia River that flows into the Pacific. They were also joined by a French-Canadian trapper and his Shoshoni wife Sacajawea, who acted as a guide.

In the spring they continued their journey up the Missouri into the Rocky Mountains before continuing on foot. The cold and wind were bitter and food ran short. But they reached the Columbia and, with help from the Shoshoni, were able to travel downstream until, on 7 November 1805, they at last reached the Pacific.

▲ Lewis wears clothes given to him by an Indian friend. He traded beads and iron pots with the people he met.

◀ Clark and Lewis pause to look at rapids on the Missouri. They decided to abandon their canoes and continue on foot.

President Jefferson rewarded Lewis and Clark with generous gifts of frontier land. Clark was appointed Governor of Missouri and held this post until his death in 1838. Lewis, who had become Governor of Louisiana, died mysteriously in 1809 while on a routine journey. No one knows whether he was murdered or killed himself.

David Thompson
(1770-1857)

David Thompson was an Englishman who went to Canada in 1784. He joined the Hudson's Bay Company, whose business was trading fur and skins. In 1790 he began to explore the Saskatchewan River, tracing its course to the glaciers of the Rocky Mountains.

Transferring, in 1797, to the North West Company, Thompson continued to explore trade routes in northwestern Canada. His most famous expedition, in which he explored the Rocky Mountains and the country to the west, left from Lake Superior in 1807. The weather was so bad that Thompson had to use all his powers of leadership to prevent his men from turning back. His team finally travelled 6,400 kilometres to cross the Rockies following the course of the Athabasca River. They were the first to cross the mountains by this route, now known as the Yellowhead Pass.

▲ Thompson was equipped, with dog-sledges, but the weather in the Rockies almost proved too much.

▼ Thompson's route across the Rockies became an important one for fur traders.

By 1812, Thompson had travelled 80,000 kilometres around Canada, and had drawn an outstanding map of the area. He eventually settled in Montreal and married a half-Indian woman; they had sixteen children. He became a strong voice in the campaign to prevent alcohol abuse in the native Indian population of North America,

Zebulon Montgomery Pike
(1779-1813)

Pikes Peak, Colorado, is a famous mountain in the Rockies. It is named after Zebulon Montgomery Pike, the explorer who was the first American to discover it.

In 1806 Pike took charge of an expedition to explore the source of the Arkansas River. This was unknown territory, and it was part of Pike's job to befriend the American Indian inhabitants of the land and claim it for the United States Government. Pike set out on 15 July 1806, and traced the river to its source close to the mountain that now carries his name. Winter was setting in, but Pike nevertheless made a brave attempt to reach the summit of the mountain, but the terrible cold forced him to turn back.

Pike then turned south to look for the source of another Mississippi tributary, the Red River, but strayed into New Mexico. This was Spanish territory and Pike was held by the Spanish. After his release, he journeyed home along a route later to become famous as the Sante Fe trail used by thousands of American pioneer settlers.

▼ When Pike entered New Mexico he was taken prisoner for several months by the Spanish. He was finally released near the American border.

At 4,300 metres, Pikes Peak is not the highest mountain in the Rockies, but it has some of the most commanding views. To the east, it looks over the great plains of Colorado and Kansas. To the south and north there are magnificent views of other peaks of the Rocky Mountains up to 160 kilometres away.

John Charles Frémont
(1813-1890)

John Charles Frémont, the American soldier and explorer, led an expedition to open up the pioneer trail to the Pacific coast, in 1842. He crossed the Great Plains, the South Pass into Colorado and the Wind River Mountains in Wyoming. The highest peak of this range is now named after him. By 1843 he had completed the trail to the mouth of the Columbia River in Oregon. Then he turned south into Nevada and crossed the mountains to the Sacramento River in California. He returned by way of Salt Lake City. When Frémont presented his report to the US Congress he was praised for his achievement. The 'Oregon Trail' was now open to allow settlers to move west.

In 1848 he led an expedition to survey the route for a Pacific railroad. This was Frémont's last expedition. He went on to make a fortune in the California Gold Rush, which his travels had helped start.

▲ As this map of 1811 shows, much of western North America was unknown to Europeans before Frémont's time. Frémont, called 'the pathfinder', paved the way for the great movement west.

Frémont's guide and companion in his 1842-3 expedition was the famous hunter and frontiersman Kit Carson (1809-1868). Carson had been an adventurer ever since he ran away from home at the age of 15. He was an expert on the old Indian trails

◀ Frémont surveys one of the mountains on his westward journey. His climb in the Wind River Mountains gave him a reputation as a mountaineer.

Isabella Bird Bishop
(1831–1904)

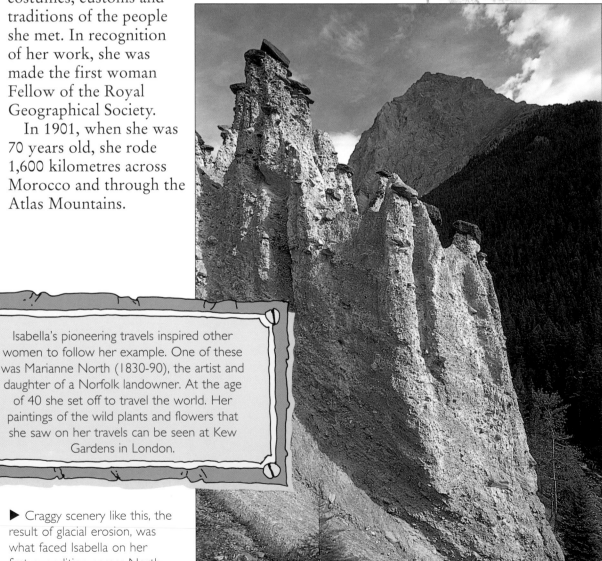

Until this century, long-distance travel was thought unsuitable for women, who were not trained to defend themselves in case of trouble. One who broke this unwritten rule was Englishwoman Isabella Bird Bishop.

She began travelling when she was 22 years old. She made a journey through North America, across the Rocky Mountains. But her real love was Asia, and over the next 25 years she travelled through Persia, Kurdistan, Tibet, Korea, China and Japan. As she went, she noted down the costumes, customs and traditions of the people she met. In recognition of her work, she was made the first woman Fellow of the Royal Geographical Society.

In 1901, when she was 70 years old, she rode 1,600 kilometres across Morocco and through the Atlas Mountains.

Isabella's pioneering travels inspired other women to follow her example. One of these was Marianne North (1830-90), the artist and daughter of a Norfolk landowner. At the age of 40 she set off to travel the world. Her paintings of the wild plants and flowers that she saw on her travels can be seen at Kew Gardens in London.

▶ Craggy scenery like this, the result of glacial erosion, was what faced Isabella on her first expedition across North America in 1853.

Luis Váez de Torres
(died 1613)

In 1605, the year in which Willem Jansz landed briefly on the mainland of Australia, a Spanish navigator, Luis Vaez de Torres, set out from Peru to find the 'southern continent' which was believed to lie in the southern Pacific. He would not have known of Jansz's landfall, although both men must have been sailing in the same area at the same time. De Torres sailed west across the Pacific from Peru. He and his crew first went ashore on the island of Espiritu Santo, one of a group of islands in the southern Pacific now known as Vanuatu. They would probably have explored the tiny island, but the crew of one of their ships mutinied. One ship went back to Peru, and the others sailed on. They went through the strait between New Guinea and Australia – later named the Torres Strait – on their way to Manila, in the Philippines, to take on stores.

Nothing more is known of de Torres's life, but one of his companions on the expedition, named de Quiros, tried to persuade the King of Spain to finance a further voyage. After many delays, permission was given – but by that time de Quiros had died.

◀ De Torres thought one of the islands of Vanuatu was much larger than it is. They named it Australia, the 'South Continent'.

▼ De Torres would have sighted the northern Australian coast when heading for the Philippines.

James Cook
(1728-1779)

James Cook, the most famous British navigator, went on his second expedition to observe the planet Venus passing in front of the sun. He sailed west across the Pacific in his ship the *Endeavour* and reached the island of Tahiti. He sailed around New Zealand and then on to Australia. In April 1770 he landed at Botany Bay – a name he chose because of the variety of plants there.

He made two more voyages. From 1772 to 1775 he sailed over 96,000 kilometres via New Zealand and the South Pacific – the first voyage to sail round the world from east to west.

In 1776 he went in search of the Pacific entrance to the Northwest Passage, but was not to return home.

It was James Cook who discovered how to conquer scurvy, the great threat to the lives of sailors on long voyages. He gave his crews daily rations of lime juice. His first expedition lasted over 1,000 days, but only one man died of scurvy during that time. From 1795 a daily ration of lime juice was given to every sailor in the English navy.

▲ On the return leg of his third journey, Cook stopped on the island of Hawaii. Some Hawaiians stole one of his ship's boats, and when Cook went ashore to recover it, he was captured and killed.

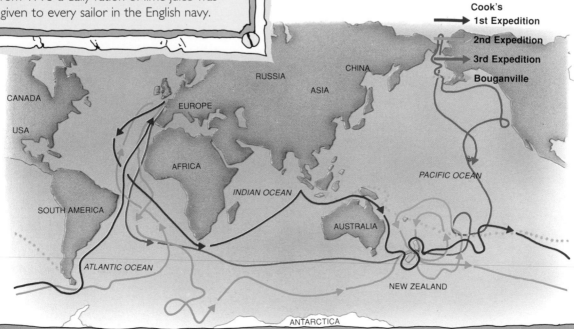

Cook's
1st Expedition
2nd Expedition
3rd Expedition
Bouganville

CHINA
RUSSIA
ASIA
CANADA
EUROPE
USA
AFRICA
PACIFIC OCEAN
INDIAN OCEAN
SOUTH AMERICA
AUSTRALIA
ATLANTIC OCEAN
NEW ZEALAND
ANTARCTICA

Louis Antoine de Bougainville
(1729-1811)

Louis Antoine de Bougainville was the first French explorer to make a voyage round the world.

De Bougainville joined the French navy in 1763 for an expedition to the Falkland Islands. In 1766 he left the Falklands with two ships. Sailing southwest across the Atlantic, he passed through the Magellan Strait and landed in the Tuamotu Islands, far out in the Pacific. After claiming these for France, he sailed on through the Pacific islands, calling at Tahiti, Samoa and the Solomon Islands. Some of the Solomon Islands had been explored earlier by Spanish sailors, but de Bougainville discovered three previously unknown ones. The largest of these is named after him. He returned to France in March 1769.

▼ Among the islands visited by Bougainville was Tahiti, where he landed in April 1768.

Bougainvillea, a tropical climbing plant of the vine family, was named after Louis de Bougainville. Its brightly-coloured clusters of flower-heads are a common feature of vegetation in tropical areas.

Fabian Gottlieb von Bellingshausen (1779-1852)

Baron Fabian von Bellingshausen, a Russian naval officer, was the first navigator to make a complete circuit of the Antarctic Continent. In 1819 he led an expedition to survey the Antarctic. With two ships crewed by 190 sailors, he sailed across the South Atlantic, carrying out a survey of the island of South Georgia on the way. When he tried to continue southwards, his route was blocked by ice.

After wintering in Australia, Bellingshausen sailed south once more.

Tsar Alexander I, who had ordered Bellingshausen's expedition, was disappointed with the results. He had expected Bellingshausen to return with a complete survey of the Antarctic mainland. The Tsar showed his displeasure by refusing to pay for Bellingshausen's maps to be printed, saying that they were too expensive.

Near to the edge of the pack ice, battling against violent storms, he discovered what he thought was part of the Antarctic mainland. Looking through telescopes from 64 kilometres offshore, he and his crew saw black rocks standing out against the ice and snow. He named this Alexander Land after the Russian Tsar Alexander I. In fact, Alexander Land is an island close to the mainland coast, but this was not discovered until 1940.

Bellingshausen also sailed close to the area of eastern Antarctica now called Enderby Land. Although he did not actually see the mainland, he noted as he passed close by that the unusual number of birds close to the ship indicated that land was not far off.

▼ Bellinghausen sailed to seventy degrees south latitude and discovered islands off the southern landmass of Antarctica. He was unable to make a complete survey of the area because icebergs like these, off Signy Island, and terrible weather conditions made progress almost impossible.

Charles Wilkes
(1798-1877)

Charles Wilkes was a junior officer in the United States navy who, in 1838, led an expedition of five ships to establish American interest in the southern seas. The party included a number of scientists including naturalists, botanists, geologists and oceanographers. Despite this, the expedition was badly planned and poorly equipped, and Wilkes confessed before he set out that he felt he was 'doomed to destruction'. The ships were warships quite unsuited to Antarctic waters. They had not been strengthened to protect them from the crushing force of the ice, and they did not have even ice-breaking tools. At every port where the ships called on their way south, men deserted.

In spite of all these problems, Wilkes' expedition sighted and mapped (though not very accurately) the northeastern area of the Antarctic, which is now called Wilkes Land after him. Generally, however, the expedition was a waste of money, and put the United States Government off further major Antarctic exploration for another eighty years.

Although the failure of Wilkes' expedition was not his fault, he was harshly treated when he returned home in June 1842. He was court-martialled, but was acquitted. Later he took part in naval actions during the American Civil War.

◀ Clues about prehistoric weather patterns and atmospheric conditions are trapped deep in the snow and ice. There are permanently manned bases in Antarctica for special scientific research.

Christopher Columbus
(1451-1506)

Christopher Columbus was born in the Italian port of Genoa in 1451 and went to sea at the age of 14. His study of maps and books convinced him that he could reach Asia by sailing westwards across the Atlantic. With the backing of the king and queen of Spain, Columbus set out in August 1492. On 12 October 1492, they sighted land.

It was one of the Bahamas, probably what is now the island of San Salvador. For the next few weeks, Columbus sailed around the Caribbean, thinking that he was somewhere off the coast of China. When he set sail for home, he left about forty men behind on the island of Hispaniola to search for gold, promising to return and visit them the following year.

Columbus kept his promise and returned in 1493 with seventeen ships and 1,500 men. But he discovered that the men he left behind had been killed by the local inhabitants. He established another colony, which survived. Later voyages took him to Trinidad and the coast of South America.

▼ Columbus's three ships, the *Niña*, the *Pinta* and the *Santa Maria*, cross the Atlantic Ocean.

It took Christopher Columbus seven years to find backing for his plan to sail to Asia via the Atlantic. He first tried King John II of Portugal, who refused. So Columbus went to Spain and put his plan to King Ferdinand and Queen Isabella. After four years of pleading, they finally agreed to pay for the voyage.

Amerigo Vespucci
(1451-1512)

Amerigo Vespucci was the explorer after whom America was named. He was a merchant and banker from Florence in Italy who went to live in Spain, met Christopher Columbus and became interested in exploration.

No one knows exactly how many voyages Vespucci made across the Atlantic. His own accounts of them are confused. The first voyage may have been in 1497. Vespucci later claimed that it was in this year that he first sighted South America, a year before Columbus did so. From 1499 to 1500 he certainly took part in a Spanish expedition with the navigator Alsonso Ojeda. During this voyage he discovered the mouth of the River Amazon. Two years later he was in South America again, exploring its Atlantic coastline southwards with a Portuguese expedition. It was on this voyage that he became convinced that America was a separate continent and not, as Columbus believed, part of Asia. To mark this discovery, the continent was named 'America' in 1507.

VENEZUELA
COLOMBIA
Negro
Amazon
PERU
BRAZIL
BOLIVIA
Parana
Uruguay
ARGENTINA
Buenos Aires

➤ Vespucci 1499
➤ Vespucci 1501–02

Amerigo Vespucci is one of exploration's 'mystery men'. He wrote differing accounts of his expeditions in letters to different friends, and the latitude and longitude positions he quoted do not always fit the facts. But Christopher Columbus never argued with Vespucci's claim to have sighted mainland South America before he did.

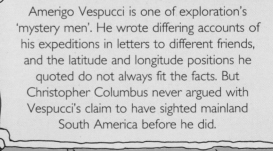

◄ The coast of Venezuela in South America was first spotted by Vespucci. He realised that it was not part of Asia, but a whole new continent.

Pedro Alvares Cabral
(c. 1467–c. 1519)

In 1500 Pedro Alvares Cabral, a Portuguese navigator, was given the command of an expedition fleet of thirteen ships. The aim of the voyage was to continue Vasco da Gama's exploration of the sea route to India. First, however, Cabral sailed southwest across the Atlantic and reached the coast of what is now Brazil. After resting, the fleet set sail eastwards, passing the Cape of Good Hope where four of the expedition's ships were wrecked in a storm. One of those who was drowned was the explorer Bartolomeu Dias.

The storm split up the fleet. One of the ships lost its way and discovered the island of Madagascar off Africa's east coast. The rest sailed on to Calicut in India, where they met trouble. Their settlement on shore was attacked by Muslim traders and many of Cabral's sailors were killed. Cabral bombarded the town from the sea in retaliation. He then sailed along the coast where he founded another settlement at Cochin, which flourished. Cabral returned to Portugal in the summer of 1501.

▲ Cabral named Brazil 'The Land of the True Cross' and claimed it for Portugal before leaving for the Cape of Good Hope.

◀ Cabral's arrival on the coast of Brazil is commemorated in this elaborate panel of decorative tiles from Lisbon.

Spain and Portugal led the world in exploration. So they signed the Treaty of Tordesillas which drew an imaginary line down the map of the world, about half-way across the Atlantic Ocean. New lands to the west of the line would go to Spain and any to the east (for example, Brazil) would belong to Portugal. This gave control of most of the Americas to Spain.

Sebastian Cabot
(c. 1474-1557)

Sebastian Cabot was the son of the explorer John Cabot, and sailed with his father's first voyage to North America in 1497. Then he worked as a mapmaker and in 1518 Charles V of Spain appointed him chief navigator to the Spanish navy. Sebastian was twice asked to lead an expedition to Newfoundland, but both times the plans fell through. Then in 1525 he was appointed to lead a Spanish expedition to Asia by the westward route.

Cabot set sail in April 1525, and by June was at the mouth of the River Plate, which separates present-day Uruguay and Argentina. Here, he met some Spanish settlers. He was so impressed with their stories of the riches to be found in La Plata, the area round the River Plate, that he decided to give up the idea of sailing to Asia and stay where he was.

He stayed in the region for three years, searching without success for riches. When he returned to Spain, he was imprisoned for three years for disobeying orders. Later, Cabot moved to England and returned to mapmaking.

For the last six years of his life, Sebastian Cabot was governor of the Merchant Adventurers, England's most important trading company. He organized three expeditions aimed at finding a way to Asia by sailing across the north of Europe.

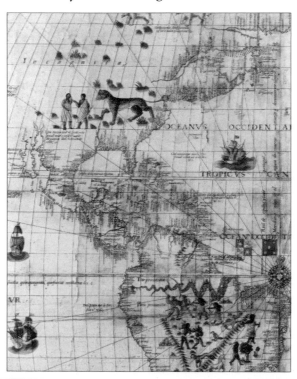

During Cabot's explorations in South America, he made friends with local Guerani Indians who gave him some ornaments made of silver (in Spanish, plata). He named the river on which they lived the Rio de la Plata, or Silver River.

◀ Cabot was an expert mapmaker, as his beautiful map of America shows. This is part of a world map Cabot made in 1544.

Francisco Pizarro
(c. 1474-1541)

Francisco Pizarro was one of Spain's most famous conquistadores . He arrived in the New World in 1504 and for a time settled as a farmer. But when he heard of the riches of the Inca empire in Peru, he decided to investigate.

With his partner and friend Diego de Almagro (see page 99), Pizarro led three expeditions to Peru. The first two, in 1524 and 1526, failed to reach the land of the Incas. In 1531 Pizarro gathered 180 men and set out to conquer Peru.

The Inca civilization was highly developed, with good roads and well-organized trade. But the Incas' only weapons were spears. They were no match for the Spaniards with their firearms. Pizarro took advantage of the quarrels within the Inca royal family. In 1532 he killed the Inca king Atahualpa. By 1533, the rule of the Incas was over and the new Spanish city of Lima had been founded. But Pizarro quarrelled with Diego de Almagro, and this led to the death of both of them. In 1538 Almagro was killed by Pizarro's brothers. Three years later, Almagro's supporters got their revenge and killed Pizarro.

▲ Pizarro and some of his companions stop by one of Petru's rivers, the Napo.

▼ The Spanish conquistadores often employed local Indians to carry their equipment.

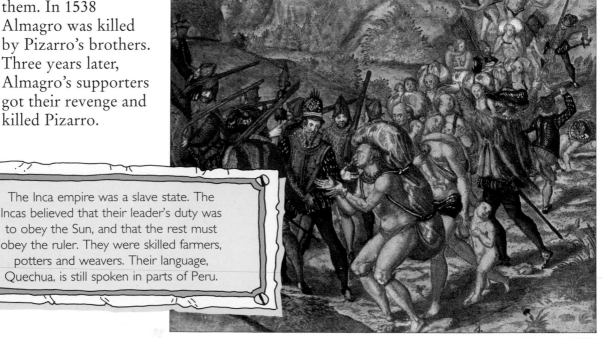

The Inca empire was a slave state. The Incas believed that their leader's duty was to obey the Sun, and that the rest must obey the ruler. They were skilled farmers, potters and weavers. Their language, Quechua, is still spoken in parts of Peru.

Diego de Almagro
(c. 1475-1538)

Diego de Almagro was Francisco Pizarro's (see page 98) partner on the expedition that led to the conquest of Peru, but he also carried out explorations on his own.

Although they had been friends, Almagro and Pizarro soon quarrelled. Perhaps this was the reason why, once the Inca empire had been conquered, Charles V of Spain tried to separate them. He made Almagro governor of the area to the south of Peru, now called Chile. This had not yet been explored by Europeans, and in 1535 Almagro led a force of 600 Spaniards and 15,000 Indians into the territory, hoping to find gold. It was a forced march over mountains in winter. Many men, suffering from frostbite, were unable to keep up and were left to die by the side of the track.

Finally, Almagro had to give up and turn back. His force returned to the Peruvian city of Cuzco in time to witness an attack against the Spanish forces by Incas. Instead of defending his fellow Spaniards – who included Pizarro's two brothers – Almagro joined the Incas and then seized the city for himself. The long-standing bad feeling between Pizarro and Almagro now turned into open warfare, which ended in 1541 with both men dead.

The old Inca way of life, before it was crushed by the Spanish conquistadores was described in a book written by Garcilaso de la Vega, the son of a Spanish officer and an Inca princess, and published in 1609. He based it on his mother's memories of her childhood in the days before the Spanish came.

▶ Pizarro's men arrest Almagro. Later Almagro was imprisoned and executed in the ruthless struggle between the two conquistadores.

Gonzalo Jiménez de Quesada
(c. 1497–1579)

Gonzalo Jiménez de Quesada was the Spanish conquistador who explored and conquered the northwestern part of South America that we now know as Colombia. In about 1535 he was appointed magistrate at Santa Marta in New Granada (the original name for Colombia). The next year he was asked to lead an expedition into the mountains, along the course of the Magdalena River in search of the fabled land of El Dorado.

It was a hard journey through dense forests and mountains. Many of the party died from illness, accidents or encounters with the Chibcha Indians who lived on the high plains. But the Spanish soldiers easily conquered the mild Chibcha people. In 1538 de Quesada founded the city of Santa Fé de Bogotá. The city is now called simply Bogotá, and is the capital of Colombia.

The Chibcha were rich in gold and emeralds and this encouraged de Quesada to think that he was close to El Dorado. At the age of 70, in 1569 he set off on another expedition to find the legendary city. The quest took him deep into the mountains of northern South America close to the borders of present-day Venezuela. In retirement, de Quesada wrote an account of his explorations, but this has since disappeared.

▲ De Quesada was one of the many European explorers of the Americas who was driven by the search for gold. Although he did not find El Dorado, he did found Bogotá, now Colombia's capital.

▼ Colombia's Mula River, with the mountains of the Sierra de Perija in the background.

The legend of El Dorado (the Gilded Man) may have its origins in an ancient Chibcha custom in which the ruler was covered in gold-dust and then plunged into Lake Guatavita to offer his riches to the gods. Stories of this ceremony may have promised of a land where limitless gold was to be found. Many conquistadores died searching for it.

Francisco de Orellana
(c. 1511–c. 1546)

The first European to explore the Amazon was a Spanish conquistador called Francisco de Orellana who had settled in Peru in 1535. In 1540 he took part in an expedition into the interior of what is now Ecuador in search of cinnamon – a valuable spice. The party was led by Gonzalo Pizarro, Francisco Pizarro's (see page 98) half-brother. The journey through the dense jungle was hard, and after many months, food began to run out. When they reached the Napo River, they decided to split the expedition in two. Orellana took fifty-seven men and a small ship that had been built on the spot in the jungle on ahead in search of food and was then to return to collect the rest of the party.

Travelling down river, Orellana reached the Amazon. He did not return, but continued his voyage, going over rapids and through regions inhabited by hostile tribes, and finally reached the mouth of the Amazon in August 1542.

▲ When travelling down the Amazon, Orellana claimed that the current was so strong that he could not turn back for his companions.

The Amazon is the longest river in South America. It was given its name because of the fierce bands of native tribeswomen who attacked Orellana's party on the river. These seemed to the travellers to be like the female warriors, the Amazons, of Greek mythology.

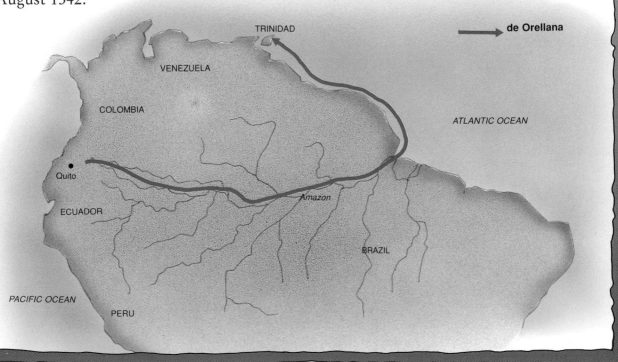

de Orellana

TRINIDAD

VENEZUELA

COLOMBIA

ATLANTIC OCEAN

Quito

Amazon

ECUADOR

BRAZIL

PACIFIC OCEAN

PERU

Walter Raleigh
(c. 1552-1618)

Walter Raleigh was an English sea-captain. He spent the early part of his career as a privateer but after hearing about the legend of El Dorado (see page 100) he led an expedition to South America, in 1595, in search of gold. He landed first on the island of Trinidad, claiming it for England and then sailed on to the mouth of the Orinoco River in Venezuela. He travelled upriver for fifteen days, then turned back and explored coastal Guyana and Surinam.

In 1617 Raleigh led another expedition to the Orinico. He was now over 60 years old, and in Trinidad he fell ill and had to stay behind. The rest of his party reached the Orinoco River, but fought with Spanish settlers there and many were killed. The expedition returned to England in disgrace. Soon afterwards, Raleigh was executed.

Earlier in his life, Raleigh had organized attempts to set up English colonies in North America. One of these was the mysterious 'lost colony' of 'Virginia' on Roanoke Island, North Carolina. In 1587, 117 settlers were landed there. Two years later, when Raleigh's ships returned, no sign of the settlers was found. They had completely vanished.

Willem Schouten
(1580-1625)

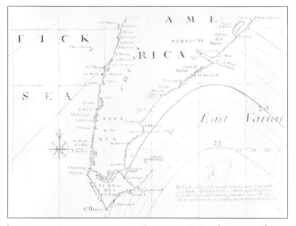

When Ferdinand Magellan (see page 9) sailed from the Atlantic into the Pacific, he went through the narrow channel between mainland South America and the island of Tierra del Fuego. This was a dangerous route, with ships in constant peril of running aground on rocks.

In 1615 a Dutch sailor, Willem Schouten, set out with two ships to discover an easier route. The Dutch were keen to use the westward passage to the Dutch East Indies. But Schouten's sailors were less enthusiastic about what was known to be a dangerous voyage. Knowing this, he kept their destination a secret for five months. When the two ships put in at a harbour in Patagonia

for repairs, one was burnt. Undaunted, Schouten sailed on in his remaining ship, the *Eendracht* (Dutch for 'unity'). Fighting against fierce storms, he rounded the southern coast of Tierra del Fuego through a channel named after his second-in-command, Jakob Le Maire. He continued westwards to the Dutch East Indies, trading with Pacific islanders as he went. When he arrived in the Indies, he was told that his trading was illegal and the *Eendracht* was seized. He and his crew had to travel home as passengers in another ship.

Willem Schouten was born in the Dutch port of Hoorn, from where he set out on his voyage. He named the southernmost tip of Tierra del Fuego Cape Hoorn (Horn) after his birthplace. Hoorn was also the home town of another famous Dutch explorer, Abel Tasman (see page 59).

▼ Cape Horn and Horn Island, surrounded by the dangerous stretch of water that many sailors feared because of rough seas and fierce storms.

Friedrich Heinrich Alexander von Humboldt (1769-1859)

Born in Berlin, Humboldt was one of the first scientist-explorers. Humboldt made two important expeditions. The first, starting in 1799, was to South America. He travelled with a French botanist friend, Aimé Bonpland. Their main aims were to study the natural history of the regions in which they travelled, and they carried a store of the most up-to-date scientific instruments. Their investigations included a study of the ocean currents off Peru (one current in this area is named after Humboldt). In a perilous river journey, they confirmed that the Orinoco River is linked to the Amazon. They also made a record-breaking climb almost to the top of Mount Chimborazo in Ecuador – at 5,800 metres, higher than anyone before had achieved. They returned to Europe in 1804.

In 1829 Humboldt went exploring again. In a six-month-long journey through Siberia to China, he studied the weather and geology of Asia, but the trip was too short to allow him to carry out the detailed studies that he wanted to.

Humboldt was convinced about the value of a worldwide chain of weather stations, and he persuaded Tsar Nicholas I of Russia to set up such stations across his empire. Other governments followed suit. Until the second half of the twentieth century, these stations were the main source of information on the world's weather.

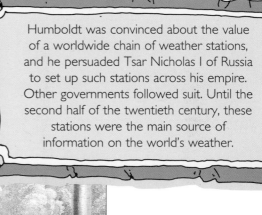

◀ Volcanic activity was one field that Humboldt could study at first hand on his voyage to South America.

Percy Harrison Fawcett
(1867–c. 1925)

Percy Fawcett was a British soldier and explorer. Born at Torquay in Devon, he joined the army at the age of 19. He became an army surveyor, and rose to the rank of colonel. In 1906 a dispute broke out between the South American states of Bolivia and Brazil over their border, and Fawcett was asked for his expert advice as a surveyor. He spent the next eight years exploring the Mato Grosso – deep in southern Brazil. This was an area of tropical climate, ferocious insects, widespread disease and hostile inhabitants.

After going to Europe to serve in World War I, Fawcett returned to the South American jungle. He was fascinated by stories he had heard about cities of ancient civilizations hidden deep in the jungle and of tribes descended from these civilizations that were said to live there still.

In 1925, Fawcett set off, with his elder son Jack and another companion, into the Mato Grosso. His expedition was well equipped, and even carried movie cameras. They were last heard of near the Kingu River, in northeastern Brazil.

▲ Dense forests and fast-flowing rivers of southern Brazil fascinated Fawcett.

▼ Fawcett meets a local tribesman in the Mato Grosso area in southern Brazil.

Fawcett's disappearance remains a mystery in spite of the efforts of a number of expeditions that set out to find him. Some heard stories that the party had been killed by hostile tribes. Others reported rumours that a white-haired Englishman had been found by an Amazon tribe and 'adopted' by them as their chief. The truth will probably never be known.

Yuri Gagarin
(1934-1968)

Yuri Gagarin, a Russian, was the first man to travel in space. He was born near Smolensk, 400 kilometres east of Moscow. In 1957 he joined the Soviet Air Force as an officer cadet and later joined the team of cosmonauts.

On 12 April 1961 Gagarin was launched into space aboard the space satellite *Vostok I*. Space technology was then very new. Gagarin spent the whole of his journey strapped into his seat. Later space travellers have been able to roam around their spaceships and even outside them. At this time it was not known whether the human body could withstand the forces needed to put a satellite into orbit, or whether the systems designed to return Gagarin to Earth would work.

Gagarin orbited the Earth, 302 kilometres from the Earth's surface. He spent eighty-nine minutes in orbit before landing safely.

▲ The rocket launched Gagarin into a 28,000-kilometre-per-hour orbit. No one knew whether he would return safely.

▼ Strapped into his seat, Gagarin had very little space inside his tiny capsule. His flight was very short, but it was the first in a series of space flights – the ultimate human journeys.

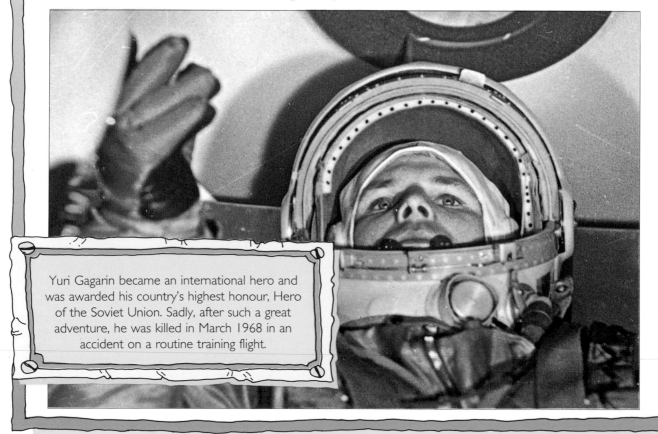

Yuri Gagarin became an international hero and was awarded his country's highest honour, Hero of the Soviet Union. Sadly, after such a great adventure, he was killed in March 1968 in an accident on a routine training flight.

Neil Armstrong (born 1930) & Edwin ('Buzz') Aldrin (born 1930)

Armstrong and Aldrin were the first two men to set foot on the Moon. Both had been fighter pilots in the Korean War. In 1962 Armstrong was chosen by the National Aeronautics and Space Administration (NASA) to train as an astronaut. Aldrin was selected a year later.

The *Apollo 11* mission in July 1969 was the first attempt to land a man on the Moon. Armstrong was the commander of the mission. Aldrin was the pilot of the lunar module, the small spacecraft that separated from the command module (main spacecraft) to make the landing. The third member of the crew, Michael Collins, a former test pilot, stayed in the command module.

▲ Neil Armstrong, Edwin 'Buzz' Aldrin and Michael Collins were the crew of the first manned mission to land on the Moon. Armstrong and Aldrin made the actual landing, while Collins orbited the Moon in the spacecraft's command module.

◄ Armstrong and Aldrin carried out various experiments before returning to Earth on 24 July.

The area of the moon where Armstrong and Aldrin landed is called the Sea of Tranquillity. They spent their time there collecting rock samples and setting up scientific instruments. One of these was a seismometer to measure movements in the Moon's crust.

Armstrong and Aldrin set foot, in that order, on the Moon on 20 July 1969. Millions of people shared this historic moment through radio and television, and heard Armstrong's words as he stepped on to the Moon's surface: 'That's one small step for a man, one giant leap for mankind.'

Fill in the blanks from the clues provided.

NO PLACE IS LEFT ON _____

_____ ENTIRELY BUT IF ____

_____ DISCOVERY, _____

_____ , THERE IS _____

A PERSON WITH _____

_____ OR A _____

_____ CAN DO – IN _____

__ _____ , _____ OR __

_____ THE _____ AT THE ___

_____ OF THE _____

_____ AND SEEK NO FURTHER

AND _____ YOU CAN ____

_____ AND BE A NAME _____

_____ TO BE _____

Clues

1 The name of this planet
2 Not known or studied
3 The reader
4 To be fond of
5 Going to different places
6 Getting knowledge of
7 A large quantity
8 To do with science
9 The same as clue 6 above
10 Connected with the science of the Earth
11 Alternatively
12 Continent explored by Leichhardt, Stuart, Burke and Willis
13 Alternatively
14 Continent explored by Hirkhouf, Hanno, Livingstone and Speke

15 Continent explored by Pizarro, Hudson and La Salle
16 Opposite of down
17 Surrounding
18 Region of northernmost latitudes
19 Highest part
20 Precise spot
21 Planet or sphere
22 Examine or search
23 Maybe
24 Obtain
25 A great idea
26 Too
27 Not at any time
28 Not remembered

Answers can be found on page 111 at the back of the book

Index

Picture Acknowledgements

The publishers would also like to thank:
Royal Geographical Society, London; British Library, London; British Museum, London; Museo Correr, Venice; Museo de America, Madrid; Metropolitan Museum of Art, New York; City of Bristol Museum & Art Gallery; New York Public Library; National Maritime Museum, London; Biblioteque Nationale, Paris; Library of Congress, Washington.

l = left, r = right
a = above, b = below

A.K.G.: 70a; 108.
Bryan and Cherry Alexander: 28a (© H. Reinhard); 31a; 37a; 39a; 41a; 70b; 77; 92 (© Paul Drummond); 93b (© David Rootes).
Ancient Art and Architecture Collection; 30a; 67b.
Bildarchiv Preussischer Kulturbesitz: 21a; 34a; 36a; 62.
Bridgeman Art Library: 8a; 10b; 18a; 19a; 19b; 20a; 25b; 37b; 46a; 48b; 49a; 49b; 52a; 72b; 74a; 75b; 87a; 94a; 94b; 97a; 102a.
G. Dagli Orti: 9a; 11a; 15b; 23a; 51a; 100a; 104a; 104b.
E.T. Archive: 9b; 28b; 33a; 33b; 52b; 60b; 78b; 81b; 91b; 103b.
Mary Evans Picture Library: 13b; 18b; 22a; 22b; 23b; 24; 25a; 26a; 26b; 30b;

31b; 39b; 40a; 46b; 51b; 56b; 59b; 61b; 64a; 65a; 65b; 66; 67a; 69a; 71a; 71b; 72a; 73b; 74b; 75a; 78a; 79a; 79b; 81a; 82b; 83; 84b; 86a; 87b; 88a; 89b; 90; 91a; 96a; 96b; 98a; 99a; 99b.
Derek Fordham:43a; 43b.
Fotomas Index:10a; 11b; 14b; 16b; 20b; 36b; 57a; 58a; 59a; 64b; 68; 72a; 103a.
Robert Harding Picture Library: 69b; 84a; (© New York Historical Society); 102b.
The Hulton-Deutsch Collection: 29a.
Hutchinson Library: 12a (© Hughes); 17b (© Tully); 44 (© Sluger); 45 (© Egan); 47a (© Errington); 47b (© Pern); 48a (© Pern); 50a (© Tully); 53 (© Dodwell); 54a (© Page); 54b (© Friend); 56a (© Friend); 76 (© Regent); 80a; 80b; 85a (© Woodhead); 85b; 86b. (© Downman); 88b (© Francis); 89a; 95 (©

Brimah; 100b (© Moser); 101 (© von Puttkamer); 105a (© von Puttkamer).
National Portrait Gallery: 17a; 32a; 61a.
Oxford Scientific Films: 55b (© Tom McHugh/ Photo Researchers).
Royal Geographical Society: 15a; 16a; 27; 29b; 38a; 40b; 55a; 57b; 82a; 93a; 105b.
Science Photo Library: 106r (Novosti); 106b (Novosti); 107a (NASA); 107b (NASA).

Front cover (clockwise)
Mary Evans Picture Library; Mary Evans Picture Library; Bridgeman Art Library; G. Dagli Orti; Bryan and Cherry Alexander; G. Dagli Orti; Mary Evans Picture Library; Science Photo Library; Mary Evans Picture Library; Mary Evans Picture Library; Bridgeman Art Library.

Back cover (clockwise)
Mary Evans Picture Library; Royal Geographical Society; Mary Evans Picture Library; G. Dagli Orti; Royal Geographical Society; Bridgeman Art Library; E.T. Archive; Robert Harding Picture Library (© New York Historical Society); Royal Geographical Society.

Introduction
Bridgeman Art Gallery: 3b; G. Dali Orti: 3l; Science Photo Library (Novosti): 3r

Puzzle (clockwise)
Bildarchiv Preussischer Kúlturbesitz; Royal Geographical Society; Royal Geographical Society; G. Dagli Orti; Mary Evans Picture Library; Science Photo Library; Mary Evans Picture Library; Bryan and Cherry Alexander.